The Complete Guide to

Understanding, Controlling, and Stopping Bullies & Bullying at Work

A Guide for Managers, Supervisors, and Employees

By Margaret R. Kohut, MSW

*Certified Criminal Justice Specialist, Certified Forensic Counselor,
Certified Domestic Violence Counselor Level III,
Master Addiction Counselor, Certified Life Coach*

The Complete Guide to Understanding, Controlling, and Stopping Bullies and Bullying at Work: A Guide for Managers, Supervisors, and Employees

Copyright © 2008 Atlantic Publishing Group, Inc.
1405 SW 6th Avenue • Ocala, Florida 34471 • Phone 800-814-1132 • Fax 352-622-1875
Web site: www.atlantic-pub.com • E-mail: sales@atlantic-pub.com
SAN Number: 268-1250

ISBN 13: 978-1-60138-236-8 • ISBN 10: 1-60138-236-7

Library of Congress Cataloging-in-Publication Data

Kohut, Margaret R.
   The complete guide to understanding, controlling, and stopping bullies & bullying at work : a complete guide for managers, supervisors, and co-workers / Margaret R. Kohut ; forward by Tina Y. Bryant.
      p. cm.
   Includes bibliographical references and index.
   ISBN-13: 978-1-60138-236-8 (alk. paper)
   ISBN-10: 1-60138-236-7 (alk. paper)
   1. Bullying in the workplace--Prevention. 2. Violence in the workplace--Prevention. I. Title.

   HF5549.5.B84K64 2008
   658.3'8--dc22
                         2008005870

Interior Layout: Vickie Taylor • vtaylor@atlantic-pub.com

Printed in the United States

Printed on Recycled Paper

Dedication

This book is respectfully dedicated to the millions of Americans from all walks of life that have been, or still are, subjected to workplace bullying who told me their stories of heartbreak and dignity.

And to the steadfast spouses, partners, children, attorneys, friends, and counselors who see them through the worst days of their lives.

Most of all, to my husband, Tristan, whose wise counsel, courage, and unfaltering devotion always make our home a soft place to fall. My love and thanks for letting me lay my world on you.

We recently lost our beloved pet "Bear," who was not only our best and dearest friend but also the "Vice President of Sunshine" here at Atlantic Publishing. He did not receive a salary but worked tirelessly 24 hours a day to please his parents. Bear was a rescue dog that turned around and showered myself, my wife Sherri, his grandparents Jean, Bob, and Nancy and every person and animal he met (maybe not rabbits) with friendship and love. He made a lot of people smile every day.

We wanted you to know that a portion of the profits of this book will be donated to The Humane Society of the United States.

–Douglas & Sherri Brown

THE HUMANE SOCIETY
OF THE UNITED STATES ©

The human-animal bond is as old as human history. We cherish our animal companions for their unconditional affection and acceptance. We feel a thrill when we glimpse wild creatures in their natural habitat or in our own backyard.

Unfortunately, the human-animal bond has at times been weakened. Humans have exploited some animal species to the point of extinction.

The Humane Society of the United States makes a difference in the lives of animals here at home and worldwide. The HSUS is dedicated to creating a world where our relationship with animals is guided by compassion. We seek a truly humane society in which animals are respected for their intrinsic value, and where the human-animal bond is strong.

Want to help animals? We have plenty of suggestions. Adopt a pet from a local shelter, join The Humane Society and be a part of our work to help companion animals and wildlife. You will be funding our educational, legislative, investigative, and outreach projects in the U.S. and across the globe.

Or perhaps you'd like to make a memorial donation in honor of a pet, friend, or relative? You can through our Kindred Spirits program. And if you'd like to contribute in a more structured way, our Planned Giving Office has suggestions about estate planning, annuities, and even gifts of stock that avoid capital gains taxes.

Maybe you have land that you would like to preserve as a lasting habitat for wildlife. Our Wildlife Land Trust can help you. Perhaps the land you want to share is a backyard — that's enough. Our Urban Wildlife Sanctuary Program will show you how to create a habitat for your wild neighbors.

So you see, it's easy to help animals. And The HSUS is here to help.

The Humane Society of the United States
2100 L Street NW
Washington, DC 20037
202-452-1100
www.hsus.org

Chapter 2: Profiles of Workplace Bullies.....35

Chapter 3: Profiles of Targets of Workplace Bullies

Foreword

"Bullies are always cowards at heart and may be credited with a pretty safe instinct in scenting their prey."
— **Anna Julia Cooper**

By Tina Y. Bryant, LMSW

If you have been, or know someone who has been, bullied in their workplace, it may help you to know that millions of Americans have also suffered from workplace bullying. There are many who will be able to identify with the contents of this book. "The Complete Guide to Understanding, Controlling, and Stopping Bullies & Bullying at Work: A Guide for Managers, Supervisors, and Employees" is especially relevant in this time of constant battles being played out in office settings every day. This guide provides poignant examples, answers, knowledge, and empowerment to those who have been bullied or are currently experiencing this abuse in their workplace. No one should be subjected to such harsh, devastating, and often illegal treatment by bosses, coworkers and subordinates that perpetuates a lifetime of emotional and physical distress upon the individual target of bullying. Workplace bullying is underreported since workers fear losing their jobs if they become "whistleblowers." Thus, it is difficult for legislators and human rights activists to develop laws and workplace policies that can eliminate this vicious behavior that is so prevalent in today's workforce.

This subject matter is noteworthy because abusive bullying of workers crosses all socioeconomic, racial, gender, and ethnic boundaries. It is based solely upon an individual's or group of individuals' attempts to hide their own inadequacies by persuading others, including upper management, to target an undeserving and usually unsuspecting individual. Their objective is to divert attention from their own shortcomings or mistakes and project it onto a seemingly innocent but vulnerable victim. Their goal is to blame, discredit, and humiliate the individual until he or she ultimately resigns or is unjustly fired, thereby resolving or covering the initial problem that led to the victimization of the target.

Bullying is exceptionally demeaning and destructive to a person's well-being. Look closely at the story of Siobhan in this book. She was an unexpected victim that had fallen prey to a gang of office bullies, destroying her career and nearly destroying her life. Fortunately, she had a level of resilience that kept her from utter destruction. Being mob bullied was traumatizing and humiliating to her and she continues to struggle in recovering from the abuse. Her family suffered as well, creating unimaginable emotional turmoil. Workplace bullying creates a domino effect that invades the lives of everyone in the victim's personal circle of friends, supportive coworkers, and family. The wounds of workplace bullying run deep and can have devastating consequences on an individual's feelings of self-worth. It deteriorates the physical and psychological being, opening the door to depression, gastric problems, headaches, insomnia, substance abuse, and a host of medical ailments. Bullying in the workplace severely damages the self-esteem and confidence of the victim, causing them to second-guess their own competence and skills. Bullying is a draining force that consumes the total person on a holistic level.

Through books like this one, the bullied individual may ultimately recognize that they are not at fault for being targeted; their vulnerabilities need not have been exploited by workplace predators. The victim is usually hand-selected to be the "fall guy" by the supervisor or group. He or she is carefully chosen to bear the burden of someone else's failures, insecurities, and pathological need to control others. The bullied individual will inevitably consider several options: to remain in the present work environment and attempt to restore a damaged reputation, to expose the bullying and seek legal action against the organization, or seek employment elsewhere and start anew. The response is clearly dependent upon the victim's perception of bullying events, and his or her capacity to advocate because of their injustice and insist upon legislation that protects bullied workers nationwide.

My hope is that this book provides understanding of the magnitude of workplace bullying, education and empowerment for all who read it, and a platform for moving in a direction to address what has affected over 23 million Americans. My goal is that readers will develop a sense of hope, endurance, and awareness as they read this book. Advocacy will prevail and laws must be developed to properly compensate those who have suffered so needlessly. If we develop our strength and tenacity over bullies, holding them accountable for their behavior along with those who condone it, our national workplace will be free from workplace bullying.

Tina Y. Bryant, LMSW

Licensed Master Social Worker

"The difference between how a person treats the powerless versus the powerful is as good a measure of human character that I know."

— Dr. Robert Sutton
The No Asshole Rule

Preface

I have been thinking about this book for more than two years. Throughout a previous book on school bullying, the issues of workplace bullying were never far from my thoughts because, like the case studies of true accounts by others found within this book, I too was the target of the cruelest and most relentless workplace bullying imaginable. Before my medical separation, I was an officer in a branch of the U.S. Armed Forces. Until my last assignment, I had an exemplary work record with the expected bumps and rough spots along the way; yet my overall job performance was something with which I could be pleased. I served my country with honor, dedication and dignity, ever attempting to polish my leadership and clinical skills.

From the day I reported to my new squadron commander at my final assignment, until the last day of my service, I was mob bullied by my group commander, squadron commander, the chief of medical staff, my immediate supervisor, and three of my subordinates. My unforgiveable sins were that I was less than perfect, I had (and still have) an informal and slightly eccentric leadership and personality style, I had never in my long career had a patient complaint unlike others, and I do not take myself too seriously; life without humor is no life at all. Three years previous to this, I suffered an episode of major depression after the suicide of my terminally ill father. This, by all later events, was unacceptable to my new superiors. Worse, I suffered from serious back pain after a duty-related incident in 2004 that required quite a bit of medical intervention.

Looking back, I believe I became a target of workplace bullying because at least one of my military superiors had a well-known history of bullying subordinates. Immediately upon my arrival at my last assignment, I witnessed him treating another member of the squadron, my subordinate, in a similar manner. Once I caught on to what was happening and tried to intervene on the target's behalf, it was too late; too late for her, and only the beginning of eighteen months of being mob bullied myself. The ending was not a happy one; I fought back for a long time, but my superior had a knack of recruiting others to pursue me as well. My long years of service ended, according to the "official version," for medical reasons. The real reason is because I could no longer find the strength to fight back. To this day, I do not know if I was mob bullied because these other individuals truly had a poor opinion of me or if they were involved due to fear of not going along with the "main bully."

With no axe to grind, I include this forward to inform readers of this book that not only did a very great deal of research form the basis of the book, but also that I have personally experienced workplace bullying of the worst sort. However, let this not blind readers to the heroic dedication of those who serve and proudly wear the uniforms of their country, putting their lives at risk every day for America's interests and way of life. What happened to me was not indicative of the character of the overwhelming majority of military personnel.

If I am passionate about ending workplace bullying, it is not for me alone, but for the millions of Americans who experience similar, if not worse, treatment by bosses, coworkers, and subordinates. Let it end now.

Margaret R. Kohut

"One who, by intentional or reckless extreme and outrageous conduct, causes severe emotional and physical distress to another is subject to liability for this distress."

— Namie & Namie
The Bully at Work

Introduction

In America alone, an estimated 23 million Americans will encounter bullying in the workplace. Most bullying is never documented or reported because until early in the new millennium, it was not fully recognized as a pervasive problem. If it was reported, it was most often dismissed as the complaints of a "disgruntled employee." Today, the tide is rapidly turning; bullied employees are weary of that label and are taking action to make themselves heard on every level from grassroots organizations to local and federal courthouses. No longer the "silent epidemic," workplace bullying is being recognized as the insidious national disgrace that it is. Employees from all parts of America's workforce and from all walks of life are, like the eccentric newsman in the movie *Network*, screaming "I'm as mad as hell, and I'm not going to take this anymore!" No longer keeping it all inside and hiding their daily excruciating emotional pain, America's bullied workers are proudly and confidently pushing the "delete" key on harassing bosses, coworkers, and subordinates through their courageous and outspoken campaign to tell the nation what has happened to them and helping to make sure that bullying in our workplaces ends with the greatest alacrity.

"In America, if you say it doesn't exist, you can keep your head in the sand. We're in total denial while bullying is ripping people's lives and health to shreds" (Namie, 2007). Workplace bullies are very skilled at what they do. They can create such internal chaos and turmoil in an employee's soul that the employee loses all perspective and sense of self; he or she begins to believe that what the bully says about them is true. Day after endless day, if employees are constantly barraged with public and/or private unwarranted criticism, poor performance reports, lack of promotions, sarcasm, accusations of incompetence, threats, and isolation, they will eventually wonder if perhaps these allegations of their lack of productive work are true. What happens next is self-doubt, depression, irrational means of attempting to cope such as alcohol or drug abuse, fury, and in far too many cases, incidents of attempted or completed suicide or fatal workplace violence.

Then comes the attempts to shift blame solely upon the stricken employee. "He's always been depressed and unstable." "Well she's an alcoholic, what do you expect?" Yet, a closer forensic behavioral analysis of a critical incident in the workplace very often reveals that the employee had no previous mental health history or substance abuse history; the critical incident occurred after prolonged and relentless workplace bullying.

Human nature has idiosyncrasies that are not easily explained. For some reason, we secretly admire bullies for their boldness, ruthlessness in getting what they want, seeming lack of conscience, and intelligent tactics. Historical bullies like Alexander the Great, the Mongol Khans, and a Roman Emperor or two fascinate and repel us at the same time. We forget George Santayana's truism that "those who cannot remember the past are condemned to repeat it," and we do. Modern-day bullies like Adolf Hitler and Saddam Hussein cease to fascinate us when reality closes in and the atrocities build. On a much smaller scale, we still seem to have this unspeakable admiration for petty tyrants while at the same time recognizing their actions as wrong, cruel, and in some cases, actionable in civil lawsuits or even criminal prosecution.

What about Hollywood's portrayal of bullies? It is safe for us to laugh at their moronic antics because we know that by the end of the movie or TV show, the bully is going to get what is coming to him or her and the "good guy" always wins in the end. Even children love fantasy bullies like Lex Luthor and the Joker because Superman and Batman always show up to save the world. Perhaps, this is one reason why workplace bullies are so overlooked; we think they can never keep up their actions for very long because, sooner or later, the hero is going to come and put an end to the whole mess.

This does not happen, according to 23 million American workers. No heroes, rescue, nor vanquishing of their bullying tormentors. To cope, they dare not cry out loud or show weakness. Tears of despair and tears of rage are saved for the long and lonely nights. Workplace bullies are like jackals; when they sense that their prey is weakening, they mercilessly stalk their victims until they prevail. Plus, it is the employee who is vanquished, often damaged beyond healing. When we ask ourselves why workplace bullying continues in today's small businesses and large corporations, the answer is clear: It continues because we allow it.

Today, as workplace bullying becomes increasingly documented and reported, there are several things that we know about this practice:

- Workplace bullying has many similarities to school bullying and domestic violence.

- Bullied employees have no "protected status" unless they are minorities or disabled.

- Bullying creates a "pressure cooker" environment that has resulted in workplace violence and other incidents.

- The label of being a "disgruntled employee" prevents targets of bullying from being taken seriously.

- Up to 80 percent of workplace bullying is done by bosses.

This book explores the aspects of workplace bullying, from the definition and scope of the problem up to and including ways to end this no-longer-silent epidemic. The case studies that are contained herein are true accounts in all respects, except that, for the purpose of confidentiality, all identifying information has been altered. In *Inferno*, Dante Alighieri wrote that the inscription over the gates to the deepest circle of hell reads, "Abandon all hope, ye who enter here." When 23 million Americans feel this way about going to their jobs each day and simply trying to earn a living, something is greatly amiss in our society that, for our betterment, and the future leaders and employees of our workplaces, must be corrected. Until, together, we too can say, "I'm as mad as hell, and I'm not going to take this anymore," we cannot call ourselves a truly noble and civilized nation.

Chapter 1

Defining the Problem

Defining Workplace Bullying

Workplace bullying is defined as the repeated mistreatment of one employee who is targeted by one or more employees with a malicious mix of humiliation, intimidation and sabotage of performance. It includes being ridiculed in the presence of other employees, being lied about to others, inducing feelings of always being on guard, not being able to focus on work tasks, loss of self-confidence on the job, out-of-control anxiety, being continually left "out of the loop," and being repeatedly criticized without just cause. Workplace bullies use their authority to undermine, frighten, or intimidate another person, often leaving the victim feeling fearful, powerless, incompetent, and ashamed.

"Every time the phone rang, I jumped. When a new e-mail appeared, I cringed in anticipation of yet another twist of the knife."

— **Susan Futterman**
When You Work for a Bully

Most targets of workplace bullying actually enjoy their jobs; were it not for the constant emotional pain and stress that results from repeated bullying, their work lives would be pleasant and productive. The bully makes this impossible through such tactics as reducing the employee's scope of authority and initiative, overloading the employee with an impossible amount of work and then chastising him or her for failing to complete it quickly, diminishing the employee's workload to menial and unrewarding tasks, constant and unwarranted oversupervision, and drastically distorting or even fabricating so-called facts about the incompetence of the employee's work performance.

Bullying rarely begins with a "bang." It tends to be a subtle process of intimidation and criticism rather than erupting in a single event. The target does not realize what is happening or what lies ahead. It is easy for the employee to say, "Oh, I'm sorry; my mistake. I'll fix it" early in the bully's game. Yet, as the weeks and months go by, the bullying not only continues, but gradually intensifies to the point of being relentless. Still, the target may not realize the true nature of the bully's actions, thinking instead that he is solely responsible for failing on the job. The bully excludes her from important meetings, condescends or patronizes her, withholds necessary information about tasks, arbitrarily changes work deadlines, bombards him with memos, e-mails and phone calls that focus on petty matters, denies him needed training, refusing to grant routine time off, habitually does not return calls or respond to memos, interrupts his work and makes unflattering — and often untrue — comments to others about his work performance. The workplace bully has no allegiance to the concept of "praise in public, criticize in private"; regardless of whether the employee is present or not, the bully will criticize in both public and private, growing ever bolder in this practice as time goes by.

Workplace bullies focus their predation on minor flaws in an employee's work, but never recognize, in public or private, good work, productivity, and the overall value of the employee to the organization. Competent managers are adept at tempering negative feedback about an employees work with praise for her positive accomplishments. The bully may offer a backhanded compliment by commenting, "Thanks for staying late to complete this, but it is unsatisfactory and needs to be reworked." The "but…" is an ever-present component of what the bully regards as a compliment. The competent, benign manager would say, "Thanks for staying late to complete this; I really appreciate your extra efforts. Let's set aside some time to discuss how I can help you improve your organization skills so you won't have to stay late anymore."

Many consider the voices of Drs. Ruth and Gary Namie to be America's premier and foremost experts on workplace bullying. Dr. Ruth Namie, a clinical psychologist, experienced intense bullying by a former supervisor. Describing workplace bullying as "a national scandal," her trauma resulted in the Namies' establishment in 1998 of the Campaign Against Workplace Violence, the Workplace Bullying Trauma Institute, and, in 2000, they hosted the first U.S. Workplace Bullying Conference. They define workplace bullying as the repeated, malicious, health-endangering mistreatment of one employee by one or more employees. It consists of psychological violence and a cruel mix of verbal and strategic assaults that prevent the bullied employee from performing well on the job. Workplace bullying, say the Namies, begins with a one-on-one aggression, but gradually escalates as the predominant bully engulfs others into mob bullying the targeted employee. It includes all types of workplace mistreatment; all harassment is bullying if it harms the target, intentionally or not.

Drs. Ruth and Gary Namie identify some startling and ominous statistics about workplace bullying:

- 80 percent of bullying targets are women

- 82 percent of targets ultimately lose their jobs

- 81 percent of bullies are bosses/managers

- 50 percent of bullies are women; 50 percent are men

- 98 percent of bullying is witnessed or known by other employees

Robert L. Mueller, an attorney, author, and expert on workplace bullying, notes it can rise to the level of a civil tort, or cause of action in a civil lawsuit for *intentional* (author's emphasis) infliction of emotional distress. This definition differs slightly, but significantly, from the Namies' definition; it indicates that while bullying behavior encompasses intentional or unintentional harm to the target, only intentional harm is legally actionable. Courts, according to Mueller, look to the intention behind bullying harassment, not just the trauma and other damages that result from it. In addition, for a targeted plaintiff to prevail, the bully's harassment must be "severe or pervasive."

Author Susan Futterman echoes Mueller's viewpoint that although workplace bullying is cruel and obnoxious, it is not illegal unless it evolves into sexual contact, physical violence, or is directed towards employees who have a "protected" status under Title VII of the Civil Rights Act of 1964, the Americans with Disabilities Act, or the Age Discrimination in Employment Act. Bullying and the law will be fully addressed in a subsequent chapter.

"My mama says that life is like a box of chocolates; you never know what you're gonna get."

— Stan Winston
Forrest Gump

Defining the Scope of the Problem

We as a society should try to understand difficult, toxic people. We are not wrong, they are. They are the ones who need to change, not us. They need to conform to society's expectations and standards of behavior. Who cares if we understand them or not?

This not-so-rhetorical question has sincere probative value; to require changes in the behavior of another person, we need to understand why they do what they do. We need not understand workplace bullies because we feel sorry for their pathology, but this type of understanding helps us, not them. In addition, we must try to understand toxic bullies because, like it or not, we will meet them on a regular basis.

A Bullying Boss

- Deviates from the employer's designated mission and

- Pursues his/her own mission for power and control over a subordinate employee

- With behaviors regarded by the community as anti-social.

— Robert L. Mueller, JD

Forrest's mama gave him some very wise advice in the novel and movie, *Forrest Gump*. We can extend this very sage wisdom into our American workplaces: When we accept a new job, we never know what we are going to get. We wonder if our boss, coworkers, and subordinates become clever, pleasant, focused on teamwork and the mission of the organization, or we will face the most vicious individual and mob bullying of our workday lives. There is no way we can predict what our future workplace environment — our box of chocolates — will be. There are some statistics that can help us understand why we need to consider the scope of workplace violence.

- One in six employees experience workplace bullying in their lifetimes.

- In terms of gender, at least 50 percent of workplace bullies are female.

- Eighty percent of bullying targets are female.

- Four out of five minority employees will encounter workplace bullying.

So wide is the scope of workplace bullying, that it has significant hidden costs to our overall workforce and economics:

- Reduced productivity, leading to reduced organizational profits

- Destabilization of the national economy

- Higher absenteeism and stress-related health problems, leading to increased health insurance costs

- Increased possibility of expensive court litigation

- Low morale among workers, leading to lack of motivation to produce

- High employee turnover rates

- Increased training costs for "replacement" employees

- Heightened potential for workplace violence

Several times in this book, attention will be called to the statistical evidence that 23 million Americans experience workplace bullying within their work lifetimes. This figure is based upon a 1999 study at Wayne State University. Targets of bullying usually feel isolated and alone; they believe that they are at fault for incompetent job performance, not realizing that millions of American workers have experienced similar workplace circumstances. Bullies are adept in making their prey feel like everything they experience on the job is their own fault. If these targets were to examine national statistics, they would learn that the scope of workplace bullying is pervasive from coast to coast.

CASE STUDY: LEA

Lea was a junior employee, age 23, in a major corporation; she joined the workforce a year earlier after specialized training. Lea was younger than most of the other company employees, but was eager to please her superiors and acquire training in her field of expertise. A few months after Lea joined the company, more senior coworkers began to critique her errors in job performance.

"I don't think they took into account that I was new, ten years younger than them, and was struggling to learn my job," Lea said. "They held me to standards that I couldn't even understand, much less complete." Lea was frequently counseled about her job performance by her immediate supervisor, who sincerely attempted to help her improve her skills. Nonetheless, Lea's higher-level supervisor targeted her for inadequate job performance while also denying her training opportunities to improve her performance on the job.

CASE STUDY: LEA

"I couldn't do anything right," said Lea. "There was one senior employee that took every opportunity to point out my shortcomings instead of helping me improve my job performance. Nothing I did was right. This person constantly complained about every mistake I made, and blew it out of proportion. She told other people that I should be fired because I drink and gamble, which is a total lie. She spread this lie all over the office just because my car was often parked at a local bar that has slot machines. If anybody had asked me, I could have told them that this place is where I play darts with my league several nights a week. I don't drink when we play because I have to drive home. See how everything I do is misinterpreted and then spread all over the place?" Lea discovered that when a new supervisor in her area was hired, her higher-level supervisor told the new boss that "I need to tell you about our problem employee," meaning Lea. She felt as if she would never have a fresh start on the job. Her new immediate supervisor objected to Lea's treatment on the job, but was silenced by the "brass" of the organization.

As the weeks and months passed, Lea began to doubt herself and her abilities, and lost hope that she would ever be able to please her superiors. She lost self-confidence and became emotionally depressed, having received no positive feedback of any kind on her job performance. Eventually, her higher-level superiors initiated job termination actions upon her, and her immediate supervisor's interventions were ignored. Lea was involuntarily terminated from her job.

"I know I'm young, and I know I'm new. I just wish I had been given a chance for training and to do tasks that I knew how to do. These people made up their minds about me before I even got started, and they never let up for one day," said Lea. "They made fun of me and called me their "problem child." How do you think that made me feel? I did my best, but nothing I did was good enough. Every time I got called into the higher-level boss's office, I knew it would be bad. My real boss tried to help me, but was threatened into silence. No one could help me. I lost my job, I have a crappy employment history and I don't know just where I'll go from here. Nowhere, I suppose. I don't want to go through this again."

Although this book specifically addresses workplace bullying in America, the term was coined in Great Britain more than a decade ago. The U.S. and the UK are certainly not alone in facing this abominable behavior; nearly every industrialized nation on the globe has brought workplace bullying into the light of day, including Canada, Mexico, India, Russia, France, Argentina,

Ireland, Sweden, Australia, and Japan. Although it may be somewhat reassuring to note that workplace bullying is not merely a matter of "Americans acting badly," it is also sobering to realize that the scope of this issue is worldwide. Nevertheless, we cannot be the masters of another's homeland, as an increasing number of Americans are demanding that bullying in their workplaces be exposed and that it comes to an end by any legal means necessary.

"Targets Don't Deserve or Want What They Get!
Workplace Bullies are Liars and Cowards!"

— Namie and Namie, 2000

Chapter 2

Profiles of Workplace Bullies

"Mad dictators don't just run countries —
sometimes they run companies."
— **Shapiro & Jankowski**

The Roots of Toxic Behavior in Workplace Bullies

There are many theories that attempt to explain the actions of the workplace bully: mental health issues, chaotic personality styles, psychoanalytic causes, learned behavior, and medical issues, to name but a few. According to Robert Hare, a prominent expert in forensic behavioral psychology, and Paul Babiak, workplace bullies *react*, rather than *act* aggressively in response to perceived provocations, slights, or insults. The term "psychopathic" refers to thoughts, feelings, and actions that manipulate, intimidate, and use others as objects to meet their own distorted goals. They note that psychopathic bullies do not feel remorse for their cruel actions toward employees, nor do they feel guilt or empathy with those they harm. By nature, they lack insight into their behavior and are thus unable or unwilling to change it. Bullies are incapable of understanding the harm that their behavior causes them as well as their targets. Thus, psychopathic bullies are particularly dangerous as "loose cannons" in the workplace.

Namie & Namie (2000) ascribe to the workplace bully a number of noxious behaviors and personal characteristics:

- A dishonest, disingenuous style of dealing with people and issues

- Plays favorites among employees

- Ensures that the target does not have the resources needed to complete work projects

- Demands that coworkers of the target provide "damning" evidence against him or her

- Uses lies, half-truths, and threats with noncooperative employees

- Assigns "dirty" tasks as punishment

- Makes nasty, rude, hostile remarks to the target; puts on a "face" with others

- Breaches the target's confidentiality; shares information with coworkers or other bosses

- Creates a "special file" about the target that's carefully kept under lock and key

Before launching further exploration of the toxic profiles of workplace bullies, a brief and easy explanation of mental health terminology will be useful for the nonclinician reader. We will often refer to the *Diagnostic and Statistical Manual of Mental Disorders of the American Psychiatric Association, Version Four, Text Revision,* or simply the *DSM-IV-TR.* This manual, now in its fourth edition, contains the descriptions and diagnostic criteria that classify all clearly defined mental health disorders used throughout the U.S. The DSM-IV-TR is divided into sections, such as anxiety disorders, childhood disorders, substance abuse disorders, depressive disorders, and personality disorders to name but a few.

In this book, we will focus primarily on the personality disorders since the great majority of workplace bullying behavior stems from these disorders. Note that personality disorders are *not* mental illnesses, differentiating them from conditions like schizophrenia, panic disorder, or major depression. Rather, a personality disorder is a pervasive and enduring pattern of internal experiences and outward behaviors that deviate significantly from behavior that is expected by society. People with personality disorders are very rigid and inflexible in personal, social, and occupational situations. "If you find yourself dealing with someone who has destructive ways of thinking and behavior, who has unexpected and/or unpredictable moods, does not 'play well with others,' and has poor impulse control, chances are you've just encountered someone with a personality disorder" (Kohut, 2004). Since personality disorders are not mental illnesses, they cannot be "cured." Those affected can learn to modify and minimize their chaotic behavior, but treatment like this is seldom successful since personality disordered individuals are in deep denial that they are not the problem. To them, other people are the problem, and it is these others who need to change, not them.

"You can't change what you don't acknowledge."
— Dr. P. C. McGraw

Some of the more interpersonally troublesome personality disorders are cited as the toxic roots of bullies in the workplace:

- The Paranoid Personality Disorder

- The Antisocial Personality Disorder

- The Narcissistic Personality Disorder

- The Histrionic Personality Disorder

- The Borderline Personality Disorder

- The Obsessive-Compulsive Personality Disorder

- The Dependent Personality Disorder

- The Schizoid Personality Disorder

- The Avoidant Personality Disorder

- "JPM" (Just Plain Mean")

In describing how personality disorders are precursors to workplace bullies, it must be clear that not only are we referring to bosses and managers, but also to toxic coworkers and subordinates. Regardless of their positions, personality disorders in the workplace are disruptive and unpredictable; managers and bosses pose special problems. Sharing a workplace with a seriously personality-disordered individual is extraordinarily stressful for many reasons:

- **They have great difficulties in interpersonal relationships**; requests are ignored, deadlines come and go, simple differences of opinion erupt into major arguments, and minor errors become mind-numbing crucial mistakes.

- **They are "ego syntonic,"** meaning that they see their pathology as a virtue and strength, rather than as seriously damaging to others in the workplace.

- **They lack empathy with others.** Individuals with personality disorders very often do not understand — or care — that they are harming others. They view their hurtful actions as "right," and if their superior, coworker, or subordinate is distressed because of their actions, that is his or her problem; they are just too sensitive.

- **They have difficulties maintaining boundaries.** Some personality-disordered people cannot maintain the interpersonal boundaries that are expected in the workplace. This is the boss who habitually and intensely bullies a subordinate, and then asks that subordinate out for a beer after work. It is the subordinate who continually undermines her supervisor, and then describes him as "my best friend."

- **They have rigid and irrational belief patterns.** This is the bully who has unshakable and nonsensical beliefs such as "I am a failure if my subordinate makes a mistake, so I have to micromanage him," "Everyone is picking on me," or "Only other talented and gifted people understand me."

- **They tend to have hidden agendas.** The organization's agenda is not their own agenda; personality-disordered people follow their own script while appearing to tout the organization's goals. "That is not the way the boss wants it done" is truly the message that "I will rephrase your work and pass if off as my own, telling the boss that I had to do it for you."

- **They lack emotional intelligence.** Workplace bullies do not understand how to respond to their social surroundings;

they cannot relate to others on an emotional level or solve conflicts or problems without becoming adversarial. They are incapable of disagreeing without being disagreeable.

- **They are "one-trick ponies."** These bullies know how to do one thing, and they do it well to the exclusion of other tasks or abilities. They have an inflexible pattern of how things should be done, and woe to the boss, coworker, or subordinate who deviates from this pattern.

Although personality disorders — or at least features of a particular disorder — dominate the root cause of toxic, bullying bosses, coworkers, and subordinates, it should be noted that not all workplace bullies have a personality disorder; some are "Just Plain Mean" (JPM). These individuals undermine and terrorize their targets to cope with their own fears of inadequacy, further their self-aggrandization, and because they have a fondness for "winning" power and control contests at work. Since personality-disorder features and the full-blown disorder are so prevalent in the workplace, it is important to understand the inner workings of workplace bullies as suggested by the most current research.

A PERSONALITY DISORDER FABLE

Once there was a snake that was trapped on one side of a lake. Then a frog hopped by and the snake called out to the frog, "Hey! Can you take me to the other side of the lake? I could ride on your back while you swim across." The frog replied, "How do I know you will not bite me?" "Why would I do that?" asked the snake. "If I bite you, we will both drown." The frog agreed, and the snake hopped on the frog's back for the ride across the lake. But halfway to the other side, the snake bit the frog. As they were both sinking under the waters, the frog cried, "Why did you bite me? You said you would not!" The drowning snake replied, "I cannot help it; it is just my nature."

The Narcissist

"Copernicus was wrong:
I AM the center of the universe!"
— Dr. Roy Lubit

Scratch the surface of any workplace bully, and chances are you will find many characteristics of the Narcissistic Personality Disorder. "It is all about ME!" is the narcissist's anthem. These bullies are self-absorbed, lacking in empathy for others, and are never, ever wrong. The DSM-IV-TR attributes the following personality features to narcissists:

- An exaggerated and undeserved sense of self-importance

- Preoccupation with fantasies of unlimited success, power, brilliance, beauty, or ideal love

- A belief that he or she is "special" and can only be understood by other special or high-status people

- The need for excessive admiration

- A feeling of entitlement such as unreasonable expectations of special treatment or instant compliance with his or her expectations

- The habit of being interpersonally exploitative; taking advantage of others to achieve his or her own agenda

- Lack of empathy toward others; unwillingness to recognize or identify with the feelings and needs of others

- Intense envy of others, or a belief that others are envious of him or her

A distinction should be made between normal, healthy narcissism and pathological, destructive narcissism. Everyone seeks self-confidence, is pleased with positive accomplishments, and instinctively seeks to meet their own needs; these characteristics are "hard-wired" into the human race for our physical and emotional protection and advancement of the species. In many situations, healthy narcissism is both expected and essential. For example, if you were facing brain surgery, you would want your neurosurgeon to be supremely confident in his or her skills in order to save your life. Fighter jet pilots in the U.S. armed services are known to have "egos." Considering what they do, their willingness to do it, and their truly extraordinary skill in doing it, these individuals must have a very hearty dose of healthy narcissism. In short, there is narcissism within us all; this is why, at least for the time being, human beings are the masters of planet Earth.

It all begins to go wrong in the workplace when a boss, coworker, or subordinate is a pathological, destructive narcissist. These individuals are very likely to be at the top of the hit parade of workplace bullies. They manipulate, scapegoat, and exploit others with no concern about the impact of their actions on their targets. Dominated by grandiosity and preoccupation with themselves, they are supremely arrogant and seek constantly to devalue others. They feel entitled to do and say what they wish; the rules of social conduct do not apply to them. Since it is impossible for them to be in error about anything, they are extremely sensitive to perceived slights and will respond with rage and a desire for retribution. They appear to have no attachment to moral or social values. In the workplace, the narcissistic bully does what he or she wants. Grandiose bullying narcissists are always legends in their own minds.

CASE STUDY: MICHAEL

"I don't understand why I'm in trouble all the time. I came to this job with a near-perfect work record at my old job. I did well in training, made promotions regularly, and as far as I know, I was well liked. Then I came here, and all of a sudden I was a complete idiot and everyone in my section disliked and resented me. At least that's what my new boss told me. I've always been confident about my work, but she hammered me every single day about stupid, minute flaws because I didn't cross a "t" or something. I can't meet her expectations, and I have no idea why."

Michael is a 39-year-old administrative assistant in a business that specializes in creating custom-designed audiovisual material for large corporations. He sought counseling services due to his perceived inability to meet the expectations of Jana, his new boss. Michael stated that Jana frequently requires him to come to work early or stay late to complete extra tasks for which he is not paid, berates him for his lack of creativity, refuses to hear his concerns about her treatment of him, and speaks to him in a haughty and sarcastic tone of voice, "Like she's talking to a child." In the six months that Michael has been working for this business, he stated that he has never received a compliment from Jana about his work, only relentless criticism. Michael believes that Jana is aware of his intense feelings of distress about their working relationships, but she appears to be unconcerned about his feelings.

"She says I'm not creative enough with the training AV material, but at the same time, it seems like I'm not allowed to have ideas, especially if I think of something that she doesn't. There's no way I can prove it, but I swear that she took one of my ideas and told her own boss that it was her idea. Of course, I'm not even worth talking to. Jana only interacts with other managers; in my section, we're just the hired help. I don't want to quit after only six months because it will look bad on my resume. I just have to stick it out."

CASE STUDY: MICHAEL

Michael had the misfortune to work for a pathologically narcissistic boss. According to his therapist, Michael was becoming depressed, suffered from chronic tension headaches and an upset stomach, and felt extremely bitter and frustrated toward Jana. Michael believed he only existed to feed Jana's ego and need for power over others; he felt as if he contributed nothing to the mission of the business.

What to Expect From the Narcissistic Bullying Boss

- You are an employee, nothing more; an object used only for work tasks. Your boss is not interested in you as a person. He expects you to keep long hours at work; if you object, expect harsh criticism for not being a "team player."

- You are expected to have brilliant ideas on demand; if you do not, expect to be criticized for lack of motivation and creativity. Your ideas must never be too good or your bullying boss will feel threatened and will increase her berating, bullying actions to demoralize you.

- If you fail, it is your fault. If you succeed, it is your boss's success, not yours.

- Never demonstrate your frustration, emotional distress, or physical symptoms of stress; the narcissistic bullying boss will peg you as unstable, pessimistic, overly sensitive and unreliable — and will let you know of her negative opinion of you at every opportunity, public or private.

- Expect to be exploited for this bully's own ends. Expect nothing in return.

- The rules of the workplace apply to you, but not to this bullying boss. He will come and go when he pleases and do what he wants; if you make the smallest of procedural errors, expect to be barraged with feedback about your selfishness and ignorance.

- The more distressed you become, the more this bully will close in on you by omitting no opportunity to point out your shortcomings to you, your coworkers, and the company's "higher-ups." You will become the workplace problem child, and there will be nothing you can do to rid yourself of this label.

What to Expect From the Narcissistic Bullying Coworker

- Company rules apply to you, but not to her. Expect this bully to report you to your supervisor if you are five minutes late returning from lunch.

- Expect to find that what is yours is his, and what is his better be left alone. If you are missing your coffee cup, your mouse pad, or your computer disks, you will know where to find them.

- You will fight your battles alone. This bully will delight in your minor conflicts with other coworkers and/or supervisor, and will make them even worse if she can. Expect no loyalty or support because it will not ever be there.

- Of primary concern to the bullying coworker is her own reputation and appearance on the job. If she has to denigrate you to make herself look good, she will do so with no hesitation, empathy or conscience.

- This bully is not interested in having your friendship and will be totally insensitive to your needs. If you confide in him about your wife's recent DUI, a child's suspension from school, or financial worries, expect him to find some way to use this information to reflect negatively upon you with your supervisor. Your problems are his weapons against him; tell him nothing.

- You are not "special" enough to warrant the narcissistic bullying coworker's attention except to manipulate and intimidate you. He has his eye on the boss's chair, and you had best not come between her and her agenda.

- Expect to keep checking to see if you have a knife sticking in your back; chances are, this self-righteous bully put it there.

What to Expect From the Narcissistic Bullying Subordinate

- He will express his undying support for you to your face, and undermine you behind your back; this bully specializes in appearing to be what he is not.

- Expect to be used for mentoring, achieving commendations and promotions, and pay raises. Expect absolutely nothing in return.

- This bully will want to get rid of you, either by your promotion so that she too can move up the ladder, or by getting you fired; she does not care which as long as you get out of her way.

- When you shine, she will be on your side. If your ship is

sinking, she will be the first one in the lifeboat, leaving you on your own.

- Expect to be bullied subtlety, not overtly. The narcissist is too smart to declare open warfare with you. This bully will quietly keep tabs on everything you do or say that could be negatively misinterpreted by your supervisor and tell all when the time is right.

In summary, the narcissistic workplace bully is a difficult, toxic, and dangerous individual to work for, work with, or supervise. They are always energetic and charismatic, and have a knack for being completely convincing in their seemingly benign concern about the "problem employee" in their midst. To an organization's higher-ups, this bully appears caring and empathetic toward this wayward employee; this appearance is a sham, a manipulation, and is actually part of a vicious and unrelenting campaign to drive out the target employee. Worst of all, the bullying narcissist can easily convince even the target employee that he or she is a worthless failure on the job.

"She's so good with her stiletto,
You won't even feel the pain…"
— Billy Joel
"Stiletto"

The Antisocial

Adolf Hitler. Ted Bundy. Charles Manson. Saddam Hussein. Four of the most vicious human monsters of modern history seem, on the surface, to have nothing to do with the profile of a workplace bully. Yet, these notorious criminals share one crucial element with corporate bullies: The Antisocial Personality

Disorder (ASPD). Fiction can be just as terrifying as real life, as evidenced by the eerie, aristocratic, and merciless killer created by author Thomas Harris: Dr. Hannibal "The Cannibal" Lecter, the perfect embodiment of the ASPD. Highly intelligent, cultured, extremely well educated and possessing a chameleon-like ability to disguise his true nature behind the mask of a benevolent and highly competent psychiatrist, Harris takes readers of his four "Hannibal" novels deep into the mind of a completely sane, yet completely pathological antisocial serial murderer (Kohut, 2004).

It is little wonder that the workplace bully who matches the DSM-IV-TR diagnostic criteria for the Antisocial Personality Disorder is the most dangerous of all bullying bosses, coworkers, and subordinates an employee would be unfortunate enough to encounter. It is not because, like history's real-life ASPDs or fearsome fictional creations like Hannibal Lecter, an employee's life is in danger, but because both types of the ASPD — the "criminal" and "sub-criminal," — share common characteristics that can make an employee's work life seem like a living hell. Forensic researcher Paul Babiak refers to the "sub-criminal" type of ASPD as a "successful industrial psychopath."

According to the DSM-IV-TR, the ASPD is characterized by:

- A pervasive pattern of disregard for and violation of the rights of others

- Failure to conform to social norms of behavior; often criminal behavior

- Deceitfulness, lying, or conning others for personal profit or pleasure

- Impulsivity or failure to plan ahead and consider consequences of their actions

- Irritability and aggressiveness

- Reckless disregard for the safety of themselves and others

- Consistent irresponsibility via repeated failure to sustain obligations and commitments

- Lack of remorse; indifferent to or rationalizing having hurt or mistreated others

The mystery of the characteristics of the ASPD is that they can exist within a merciless serial killer like Ted Bundy, as well as within an organization's CEO or an employee's boss, coworker, or subordinate; the characteristics are simply expressed, or acted out, in a different manner. According to forensic behavior expert Robert Hare (1993), "white-collar psychopaths" are a subtype of the ASPD. Note the terms "psychopath," sociopath," and "ASPD" are often used interchangeably. Babiak and Hare (2007) make the point that the majority of prison inmates meet the diagnostic criteria for ASPD, but this does not mean that all ASPDs are criminals. We find them just as easily in an organization's board room as on death row. The ASPD's natural charm, wit, and intelligence help them appear to be excellent candidates for leadership positions in businesses, for promotions and raises, and as public representatives of a workplace. Even if job interviewers are fooled by the ASPD's mask of benevolent civility, in the actual workplace, an employee unfamiliar with this clinical diagnosis instinctively knows that something is seriously amiss with a boss, coworker, or subordinate. The merciless viper in their midst is the antisocial workplace bully.

Barbarians at the Gate: Antisocial Bullies in the Workplace

ASPDs manipulate others and break rules of acceptable, pro-social conduct because it provides them with a thrill; simply, they enjoy it. They find a sense of satisfaction in getting away with hurting others. Employees find that these individuals are not at all constrained by normal inhibitions to avoid harming others; they only become anxious about their behavior and the employee's reaction if they are about to be caught. If this occurs, the ASPD will blame others, make excuses, express no remorse, and make frequently successful, convincing arguments to superiors that the targeted employee is at fault, not them. Although these bullies may express remorse when they are "nailed" for bullying an employee into unbearable distress, the ASPD boss, coworker, or subordinate is about as capable of feeling genuine remorse as the snake in the previous fable was of not biting the frog; it is just not their nature. Even if there are many theories about the genesis of the ASPD, such as "nature vs. nurture," it is clear from the research that while the vast majority of people express a genuine conscience and empathy for others, the antisocial individual never develops this personality trait. Thus, for the bullied employee, it is impossible for the antisocial to change. In the workplace, the ASPD bully must be coped with cleverly and consistently for other employees to work for or with them without suffering what appears (and is) their nature to hurt and exploit others.

What to Expect From the ASPD Boss

Dr. Roy Lubit (2004) wrote that the antisocial superior is particularly dangerous, sometimes to the point of wanting a subordinate employee to break company rules and/or engage in unethical, even illegal conduct. The employee that refuses to compromise his or her ethical standards will immediately become a target of relentless bullying for having dared to refuse the antisocial boss. Rather than admire the employee's integrity (this is a foreign concept to the ASPD), this bullying boss will regard the employee's refusal as a sign of weakness. In a company of section run by an antisocial boss, "weak" employees do not last long. Lubit's advice is simple: stay away from them if at all possible. If the antisocial boss self-destructs when confronted by superiors, this bully will take everyone around him or her down, too.

Expect to feel abused, humiliated, and powerless; the ASPD boss evokes all these feelings in a targeted employee. In the movie *Rocky III*, boxing heavyweight champion Rocky Balboa was confronted with the daunting task of a match with the formidable, very intimidating Clubber Lang; in a prefight news conference, Lang was asked to predict what Rocky could expect from the match, to which Lang replied, "Pain." Employees who work for a bullying ASPD boss will soon feel as if they have gone 13 rounds with Clubber Lang.

LESS THAN 50 WAYS TO LEAVE YOUR BULLY
(APOLOGIES TO PAUL SIMON)

1. Make a new plan, Stan.	7. Tell him you're gone, John.
2. Drop off your key, Lee.	8. Say she is a pain, Jane.
3. Jump on the bus, Gus.	9. Complain to his boss, Ross.
4. Never look back, Jack.	10. Get a new job, Bob.
5. Pack up your desk, Bess.	11. You don't need to be coy, Roy....Just get yourself free!
6. Laugh in her face, Grace.	

— **Susan Futterman and author**

For employees who like their jobs, have trained extensively to perform them well, and do not wish to knuckle under to the bullying psychopath, survival is possible as will be discussed in subsequent chapters on coping, and even prospering, despite working for this type of boss.

CASE STUDY: VERONICA

"My boss told me to do something that I knew was professionally unethical; I made the horrible mistake of saying 'no' to him. At least, it felt like a mistake at the time, but now in hindsight I know I was right." Veronica worked for a large organization for nearly 17 years. In her 15th year on the job, she was transferred to a new location within the same organization.

Her new boss seems cordial, interested in her leadership of her section, and complimentary of her outstanding work performance history. This cordiality continued between them until her boss told her to treat a client of the company in an unethical and potentially harmful manner. Respectfully, Veronica told her boss that she could not comply with his instruction, for ethically sound, well-thought out reasons. Although her boss appeared to accept her response, from that day on, Veronica found herself the target of the boss's subtle but professionally and emotionally devastating bullying.

"He took every opportunity to undermine me with his superiors, my coworkers, and even my subordinates. He spread lies about my mental stability, my total lack of leadership in my section, and alleged work-related errors that had no foundation in truth. He twisted everything I did or said to reflect negatively upon me. I was constantly called into his office to be counseled or reprimanded for the minutest flaw in my performance. All this went into my official work record, making my chances of promotion disappear forever. Every day it seemed like I became more and more stressed. I couldn't sleep, I couldn't eat, I cried all the time at home, and I finally was placed on anti-depressant medication by my doctor."

"Still, it went on. I was the very public target of being publically disgraced. I

CASE STUDY: VERONICA

was eventually removed from my leadership position and reassigned to silly, meaningless 'busywork.' My boss knew how distressed I was because I told him — a bad mistake — and because my absentee record increased due to having to see a mental health counselor that the company paid for. He couldn't care less how much he hurt me. In fact, I think he liked it, especially when he 'converted' many of my coworkers and subordinates to his point of view of me as a complete failure. One day at work, I just lost it. I shut my office door and sobbed. I wouldn't let anyone in because I didn't want to be seen this way. He finally used his own key to come into my office and chastise me for being "too emotional." I couldn't believe his lack of caring; he knew full well that he did all this to me, and then blamed me for it. He initiated termination proceedings against me for being unstable and incompetent. I fought this for a long time as hard as I could, but he held every card. The most bizarre thing of all was when he came to my office, berated me for my failure on the job, and then told me that 'when all this was over, we need to go out and drink beer together; you like beer, don't you?' That did it. I stopped fighting and quit three years before I was eligible for retirement benefits. A supportive friend told me that the boss was going to fire me on my birthday in two months. It was no longer a question of money and reputation; it was a question of survival."

"Would Charlie Manson have been able to convince his followers to commit murder had it not been for the charismatic charm and power he held over them? So, too, the sub-criminal psychopath often possesses a remarkable charismatic charm."

What to Expect From the ASPD Coworker

Watch your back. Like the Narcissistic coworker, the ASPD colleague can fatally wound an unwatchful employee easily and efficiently. While displaying cordiality, teamwork, and support when others are around, this bully can win the battle before the employee even realizes he or she is involved in a war. The camaraderie disappears once the bully no longer has an audience, and the unsuspecting employee finds all the work piled on her desk, needed supplies and documents have disappeared, important clients' accounts have inexplicably been transferred to the oh-so-pleasant bullying coworker who has called in sick — again. These bullies either have very few limits and boundaries, or they habitually cross well-established boundaries. They will invade an unlocked desk, non-password protected computer, and purses or briefcases left in plain view. They will invite a targeted employee to lunch and even pick up the tab, and an hour later appear in the boss's office with a barrage of complaints about the employee's lack of competence. The ASPD coworker is nothing if not thorough and clever; if the targeted employee were to turn the tables and raid the bully's desk, it would not be unusual to find a dossier of written memos that document the target's every move, always putting a negative spin and unflattering twist on the target's actions and conversations. The employee unwittingly becomes an accomplice against himself or herself; a housefly does not notice the spider's web until it is hopelessly and fatally entangled.

This bully loves to dish the dirt. A targeted employee who has a brief moment of tears for a very ill family member or friend will be labeled as unstable. Seen having a pre-dinner cocktail results in being designated as an alcoholic. A friendship with a coworker of the opposite gender becomes an extramarital affair. Using the petty cash to buy a box of printer paper becomes embezzlement. A friendship with a same-gender friend becomes a gay affair. If it can be twisted into something unflattering and sinister, expect the ASPD bullying coworker to be right on top of it, and will not think twice about using it to discredit the targeted employee with no regard for either the truth or the target's future in the workplace.

"Dirty little secrets, dirty little lies
We've got our dirty little fingers in everybody's pies
We love to cut you down to size
We love dirty laundry.
We can do the innuendo, we can dance and sing
When it's said and done, we haven't told you a thing
We all know that crap is king!
Give us dirty laundry..."
— Don Henley
"Dirty Laundry"

What to Expect From the ASPD Subordinate

Alan Cavaiola and Neil Lavender wrote that there is probably no workplace situation that strikes fear into the hearts of middle managers and CEOs more than having an ASPD subordinate. These subtle and meticulous bullies appear whole-heartedly devoted and loyal to the company's mission and the leadership of their immediate supervisors. They are charming and make good impressions on staff and clients alike, and do a great job of convincing the targeted employee that "I am here for you." They also scratch the surface and expect to find that the bully falsified his timecard, plagiarized the ideas of others, failed to complete tasks and blamed it on the target, secretly informed important clients about "what is really going on," and spread a very unflattering and untrue rumor about the targeted manager that ended his or her hope for an upcoming promotion. Americans living in the Southwest know that the deadly copperhead snake is often undetected until it is stepped on; it lies in wait for the perfect moment in which to strike, and it is always fully prepared to devastate its prey. A similar situation exists with this type of bully.

CASE STUDY: ROWENA

"I couldn't believe it. I wouldn't have believed it except that I saw it with my own eyes. I was called into my boss's office and presented with a written reprimand and a four-page-long document that detailed every tiny misstep that I took, every careless word, and all sorts of negatively interpreted incidents.

"According to the document, I took a personal call from my sister who, by the way, had just had a miscarriage, and I sat down in front of the fan when the office was empty and the air conditioning was broken so I wouldn't pass out from heat exhaustion. The thing that just made my jaw drop was that the first entry was dated on my very first day on the job because I wore a pantsuit to work instead of a dress that I later find out was required. I know who wrote it because he gave me an uneasy feeling from the moment I introduced myself to him as his new supervisor. I should have trusted my instinct. He kept this ongoing dossier on me for months, and I never saw it coming. I knew he came across as fake sometimes, but I had no idea that he would go to this length to hurt me. He knew he was harming me and he did it anyway. Now I'm on probation at my job; for what?"

When Rowena related this story to her supervisor's boss, she still did not understand that she had been the target of an ASPD subordinate. She had no previous experience with workplace bullying or antisocial individuals, and never made the connection. Her own intact mental health prevented her from understanding this type of workplace pathology, especially by a subordinate. Fortunately, Rowena's story had a happy ending; the written reprimand by her supervisor was removed from her file because not only were the allegations it contained unfounded, Rowena was never given a chance to respond. Her subordinate was transferred to another section, "to just become someone else's problem," Rowena concluded.

Never Underestimate the ASPD Bully

Cavaiola and Lavender pull no punches when it comes to the sub-criminal antisocial in the workplace, referring to them as the most insidious and dangerous individuals prone to wreak havoc and pain with their bullying tactics. At the highest level, white-collar crime is very lucrative, and federal prisons for ASPD embezzlers, bank defrauders, and assorted cons have good food, jogging tracks, and movies for their famous, privileged inmates. A stay at "Club Fed" is not much of a deterrent for antisocial white-collar criminals. All this fails to take into account the antisocial store clerk who bullies a new employee to the point that he or she considers suicide, or the shift manager at a fast food restaurant who is victimized and bullied by a subordinate who falsely accuses him of sexual harassment to get even with him for not putting her on the day shift. ASPD workplace bullies are not always easy to spot until they strike. Many targets make the error of assuming that "no one would go that far," or seriously underestimate how far this bully will go to harm others, break the rules, and further their own agendas. Paranoia and constant suspicion create a very unpleasant work environment, but employees can avoid falling into the trap of the ASPD by watching what they say and to whom.

"He who accepts evil without protesting it
is really cooperating with it."
— **Dr. Martin Luther King, Jr.**

"Double Trouble": The Antisocial Narcissist

A clinical description of this individual is not contained in the DSM-IV-TR. Academic research and scholarly journal articles are scarce. Yet, every employee who works with or for these people has felt the merciless force of the antisocial narcissist. As dangerous as both NPDs and ASPD are, the combination of these personality characteristics produces an individual so insidious and completely remorseless that his or her behavior sets up the workplace for intense harassment, discrimination, assault, suicide gestures and attempts, completed suicide, and homicidal workplace violence by the targets of these superpredators. Individuality is not tolerated. No one is equal to, much less better at the job, than the antisocial narcissist.

It is possible for someone to be diagnosed with more than one personality disorder. It is also just as possible for someone to not meet the clinical diagnosis of one or more personality disorders, but have traits or features of several disorders. In the workplace, it makes little difference what clinicians say; employers and employees are in great emotional and even physical danger from the antisocial narcissist.

> *"All people have the right to be equal,*
> *and the equal right to be different."*

As a boss, the antisocial narcissist selects a target that is somehow vulnerable; young, newly trained and hired workers, those with mental health issues such as being in recovery from depression or substance abuse, the insecure worker, or a worker who is different in some way that annoys this bullying boss; these bullies will not tolerate difference. Vulnerable, different, and assertive; employees who possess these three personality traits find that if they dare say "no" or disagree with the antisocial narcissist in their midst, in the slightest degree, they become targets of the most relentless campaign of destructive bullying imaginable. While these bosses are particularly difficult to deal with because of their positions of authority and power, coworkers and subordinate antisocial narcissists come very close to matching a boss's reign of terror. Actions of antisocial narcissists include:

- Constant verbal and written barrages of reprimands challenging the target's competency, stability, sobriety, honesty, and morality.

- Blatant discrimination based upon age, gender, sexual preference, or ethnicity.

- A charismatic personality style that inspires initial trust by employers, coworkers, and subordinates that often shields this individual from others' beliefs about his or her vicious nature.

- Continual violations of personal and emotional limits and boundaries, e.g., unwanted semisexual touching, and inappropriately inviting casual or intimate relationships.

- Inability to rationally accept differences of opinion; they have to "win" and have no concept of disagreeing without becoming extremely disagreeable.

- Gradual escalation of bullying behaviors, eventually creating such emotional pain for the target that self-harming behavior of some sort is likely.

- Personal and professional exploitation, intimidation, and terrorizing of targeted employees.

- A complete lack of remorse for their actions that cause traumatic physical and emotional harm to their targets.

> *"Doesn't he know that he's about to*
> *have a corpse on his hands?"*
> **— Target of an antisocial narcissist**

Antisocial narcissists greatly increase the probability of litigation by targeted employees for harassment, libel, slander, assault (sexual touching), and wrongful termination. Entire books can be devoted to bullying antisocial narcissists in the workplace, especially within the specific topic of workplace violence. For the purposes of this book, let it suffice to say that these individuals are the degenerate epitome of workplace bullying. If they are unmasked by higher-ups in the organization, immediate steps must be taken to remove them from the workplace before disaster strikes.

The Paranoid

Though not as dangerous and lacking in empathy as narcissists and antisocials, the paranoid in a workplace is exceedingly puzzling because his sense of reality is so strangely distorted. A clear distinction must be drawn between psychotic delusional paranoia and the Paranoid Personality Disorder. In psychotic mental illnesses like schizophrenia, paranoid delusions are irrational and unreal beliefs that, despite all evidence to the contrary, the schizophrenic continues to believe. These delusions are bizarre in nature: the CIA has planted listening devices in his car, space aliens are controlling her thoughts, people on TV and the radio are talking directly to him, her neighbor is conspiring to steal all the bricks from the chimney, etc. These psychotic delusions are accompanied by hallucinations: he sees things that no one else can see, she hears voices telling her to harm herself or others, he feels bugs crawling on his skin, etc. Schizophrenia, paranoid type, is a devastating brain disorder than can be controlled with antipsychotic medication. Distortions of thinking are not the same as psychotic delusions.

The Paranoid Personality Disorder (PPD) does not involve psychotic delusions or hallucinations. Like any personality disorder, the PPD is a character-related condition involving several distinct features. The DSM-IV-TR includes these PPD symptoms:

- A pervasive distrust and suspiciousness of others

- Suspicion, with no basis, that others are exploiting, harming or deceiving them

- Preoccupation with unjustified doubts about the loyalty and trustworthiness of others

- Reluctance to confide in others that information will be maliciously used against them

- Reading hidden and/or threatening meanings into mundane events or remarks

- Bearing grudges, unforgiving of perceived insults or slights

- Perception of attacks on their character or reputation; reacts angrily to these "attacks"

- Recurrent, unwarranted suspicions regarding the fidelity of a spouse or partner

The paranoid's world is a lonely one, where no one can be trusted and all others have malevolent feelings and intentions toward them. In their way, they can be frightening because of their groundless beliefs about the motives of others to harm them. A paranoid boss, coworker, or subordinate is frightening also because of the unpredictability: they can turn a friendly "good morning" comment into a suspicion about "why is he being so nice to me?" A PPD's life is filled with beliefs that they are being, or about to be, used, exploited, lied about, physically harmed, plagiarized, stolen from, and betrayed. The PPD may believe that another member of the workplace has stolen his or her ideas, but a psychotic delusional person believes that the other individual can read his or her thoughts in order to steal an idea.

PPDs see the world as a dangerous place, so they are constantly on edge and hyper-alert so as not to be taken by surprise. Since they constantly feel threatened by others, they can strike out quickly at others by false accusations and blaming. They are hostile, sarcastic, irritable, very secretive about their lives, often argumentative, jealous of others' success, arrogant, aggressive egotistical, and hypersensitive to real or imagined criticism. With this type of emotional and behavioral structure, PPDs can decompensate rapidly when their deep-seated anger, suspicion, anxiety, and resentment of others boil to the top. Among all the personality disorders, the paranoid is the one most likely to engage in workplace violence due to their "I will get them before they get me" and "I will show them!" belief system. Unlike the ASPD, the PPD becomes physically aggressive or homicidal not because they enjoy inflicting misery on others, but because they are filled with rage and have run out of options.

What to Expect From the PPD Boss

Suspecting everyone up and down the chain of command of malevolent motives, the PPD boss will use bullying tactics as a preemptive strike to prevent upstart coworkers and subordinates who do not know their place from unduly poisoning the higher-ups' minds against them. Bullying is merely a way to let coworkers and subordinates know that they are being watched, and that they are not getting away with all their schemes to undermine and cause trouble for this boss. Betrayal and disloyalty, though common, will not be tolerated. If a subordinate truly wishes to do well on the job and is ambitious for all the right reasons, the PDD bullying boss will construe this as sneaky competition to take over a work section or company. Thus, coworkers and subordinates who work with and for this bully are truly afraid to do well on the job, since the consequences of good performance are not rewarded, but punished. The PPD boss is uncomfortable with the higher-ups in an organization because he or she feels inferior to them; this bullying boss gets along best with subordinates and coworkers who come across as dependent and compliant.

CASE STUDY: ZANDER

Zander was 19 years old when he went to work at a well-known fast food "burger place" one summer to earn money for his college tuition in the fall. He had had similar jobs before in high school and was always well liked by his shift supervisor and coworkers.

He would habitually start at minimum wage, but quickly work his way through several raises during previous employments. Zander began this job in late May on the busy dinner-hour shift, and was assigned as a sandwich cook since he had experience in this area. One evening, when his shift was over, Zander noticed that the shift supervisor's office was empty, but the door was opened wide; this was against company policy since this was where each shift's cash was counted and stored by the supervisor. Concerned, Zander sought out his supervisor, Gene, and respectfully informed him that the door to his office was open. Gene immediately denied leaving the door open and told Zander, "I'll get to the bottom of this."

Zander felt alarmed; he had not meant to cause Gene or anyone else a problem. "He just went crazy," Zander said. "In front of customers at the front counter, Gene went around asking every employee if they had somehow gotten a key to his office and left the door open to make him look bad.

CASE STUDY: ZANDER

The location manager was due to make her nightly drop-in any minute; Gene was lucky I noticed the door was open so he could shut and lock it before she got there or he would have had some explaining to do. It could have cost him his job."

"Anyway, Gene went after the deputy shift supervisor, accusing him of opening the door when the boss was on her way. There is no way the deputy had a key to the office; Gene had the only key. He made the deputy empty his pockets right then and there, and then searched his locker right in front of everybody. He loudly said that the deputy was trying to get him fired so he could move up, and anyone who was in on it would get what was coming to them. Then the boss got there and everybody shut up."

"We thought that was the end of it; Gene was pretty weird at times but it blew over. But the next night before shift change, Gene called all the dinner crew in and said that he knew what we were all up to and that we were not going to get away with it. He said 'I'm in charge here, and if you don't like it, get the hell out.' After that, it was hell to work there. Days off were cancelled, Gene said nobody did their job right and he would come and do it himself, he checked that stupid door ten times a night, and no private conversations were allowed during breaks; Gene was always walking around listening. A new girl who really needed money for school only lasted two weeks before she quit because she was afraid of Gene. I needed the money too, so I stayed all summer. Never again, man."

Bullying PPD bosses terrorize workers and interfere with the business and mission of the company. They are not often promoted into higher positions because of their reputation for being odd and disagreeable. Of course, they blame sabotaging coworkers and subordinates for their lack of promotions, proof positive that they are plotted and planned against on a routine basis. The PPD boss rarely shares necessary task-related information with coworkers or subordinates, preferring to keep the information secret just in case someone should use it to do well with a task which was the intention of the information in the first place.

Frustrating, strange, irrational, and unpredictable, the bullying PPD boss is a constant source of stress within the workplace.

What to Expect From the PPD Coworker

If working for a PPD bullying boss is frustrating, the PPD coworker is downright maddening. Employee coworkers tend to have more "face time" with each other than with the boss, and sharing a work section with a paranoid can take away all vestiges of camaraderie, teamwork, and overall pleasantness of a work day.

CASE STUDY: LILY

"I'd been working in my section for about a year," Lily related to her union representative. "Last winter I had the flu really bad and was absent from work for a week, paid sick leave. On my third day off when I was still really sick, my little dog suddenly was paralyzed from the waist down. I panicked and, sick or not, rushed with her to the vet's office. She had immediate surgery for ruptured disks in her back that were causing her paralysis. It was a long, hard surgery, but she came through."

"Two days later, still half-sick, I brought her home and took good care of her. I went back to work three days later; my dog was confined to her crate and I went home at lunch to care for her. Later that week, the boss called me into her office and said that Dwayne, my coworker, had complained that I had made up a story about having the flu and about my dog being paralyzed.

"Why in the world would I do something like that? My boss said that while I was out sick, a project that Dwayne and I were working on together came due and not only was it late, but it was sloppy, too. Dwayne said that I did this on purpose so he'd have to do the job by himself. He said I knew he couldn't do it alone and that I wanted to make him look bad and embarrass him in front of everyone."

CASE STUDY: LILY

"That's stupid! He also gave the boss a list of things I had supposedly done in the past several months that undermined him and criticized him. He never once asked how I was feeling and how my dog was doing. I got a letter from my doctor to prove that I had the flu, and I took a picture of my dog's back all full of horrible black stitches and gave it to my boss. Then I took a copy of the picture and just quietly put it on Dwayne's desk. My friend in the section told me that Dwayne started talking about how pictures can be faked, like in the movie *Forrest Gump*. He just wouldn't let it go. I ended up re-doing the project and when the boss complimented me on it, Dwayne told me to my face that I'd planned this all along to get ahead. Every time I watch my little dog up and walking around again, I just want to strangle Dwayne."

Lily's story is not uncommon with a bullying PPD coworker stirring up the workplace. They are grandiose about their ability to figure out all the underlying schemes in a section, most of which are aimed at them. Nonetheless, they are smarter than these schemers and are constantly hyper-alert for any hint of malevolent intent or actions by their coworkers. They bully others through false allegations of elaborate plots against them, taking what action they can to prevent a coworker's advancement, blaming others for their mistakes, and spreading untrue rumors about a target coworker's "connections" with the higher-ups. Unlike the narcissist or antisocial bullies who know that their allegations and rumors are false, the paranoid bully believes that they are true, and the office is entitled to know just what a scumbag the target employee truly is, despite his or her good reputation.

What to Expect From the PPD Subordinate

When a manager acquires a new employee that shortly begins demonstrating paranoid beliefs, it will not take long before the manager says to himself, "Here comes trouble" when this subordinate asks for a private conversation. The PPD subordinate is difficult to supervise since he or she is hypersensitive to necessary corrective feedback that the subordinate, naturally, views as untrue and as part of a plot to get her fired during her probationary period. Feedback that is appropriately accepted by other employees is viewed as a major slight and humiliation to the paranoid. Managers know that they must take a deep breath, remain calm, and expect the worst when it is time for this subordinate's performance review. The PPD subordinate bullies the manager by vehemently disputing anything but a perfect performance evaluation, threatening to call a lawyer to file a harassment lawsuit, threatening to report the manager to the labor union, accusing the manager of disliking him and playing favorites within the section. This type of subordinate bullies both immediate supervisors and higher-ups by wearing them out with threats, complaints of rampant schemes against them, barraging them with memos, e-mails and documented "proof" that she is an innocent and highly competent victim of others in the workplace. A manager may walk on eggshells around this bully so as not to set off a chaotic, grandiose period of intolerable workplace conditions. This, in turn, causes anger and frustration by the manager and coworkers toward the PPD bully since he is getting away with his blustery, inappropriate behavior instead of being assertively counseled by the manager. Finally, when everyone has had enough, the PPD subordinate is fired not for poor work performance, but for being a disruption in the section. "See?" this bully will declare, "I knew you were out to get me from the start, and this proves it. Now you're really going to hear from my lawyer. See you in court!" Never mind that the bully does not even have a lawyer; a savvy attorney can spot in a moment that this individual is bad news and was terminated for good cause. It is this bully's constant paranoid ideation that is wearisome, not necessarily his or her job performance. As a result, a manager may choose to regard the PPD subordinate bully as a "necessary evil" and focus upon keeping peace at any price.

Narcissist: "I'm better than you because I'm smarter and more creative."

Antisocial: "I'm better than you, and I'll hurt you to prove it."

Paranoid: "I'm better than you, that's why you steal all my ideas."

The Histrionic

Drama, drama, and even more drama; that is what the Histrionic Personality Disorder (HPD) is all about. If there is some kind of high emotion in the workplace, such as an impending unit inspection, the histrionic will without fail create more tension and chaos than that which already exists. If the workplace is stress-free and congenial, the histrionic will come up with some real or fictional drama to stir the pot and make sure it stays stirred; the lack of drama is intolerable to the HPD employee, both personally and professionally. The term "disorder" not only clinically describes this individual, but it is also what he or she creates on the job — as much disorder as possible.

The DSM-IV-TR describes these characteristics of the Histrionic Personality Disorder:

- Uncomfortable in situations where he or she is not the center of attention

- Interacts with others in inappropriate sexually seductive or provocative ways

- Displays rapidly shifting and shallow expressions of emotion

- Uses his or her physical appearance to draw attention

- Has a style of speech that is excessively impressionistic and lacking in detail

- Self-dramatization, theatricality, and exaggerated expression of emotions

- Easily suggestible and influenced by others or circumstances

- Considers relationships to be more intimate than they actually are

"In my section, we like and respect each other and have good senses of humor, except for just one person who rained on everyone's parade. At our holiday party and gift exchange, the subordinate who drew my name took away the funny T-shirt he gave me to exchange it for a smaller size. I laughed and called him and Indian-giver. My paranoid subordinate was a full-blood Native American who promptly filed a discrimination complaint against me. I realize I should have been more politically correct, but I never discriminated against her because of her ethnicity. The discrimination complaint was dismissed, but I was verbally counseled by my boss to watch what I say around her since she tended to cause trouble for managers she doesn't like."
— Manager of a PPD subordinate bully

Histrionic individuals are very tuned-in to their immediate circumstances and are adept at "reading" people to find out what type of behavior is required of them in order to secure the spotlight squarely upon themselves. So fearful are they of rejection and abandonment that they will become whatever they need to become to insert themselves as the center of attention of every situation. Gaining reassurance that they are accepted and admired is the HPD's agenda; without this, they can become overwhelmed with panic and anxiety. Within this context, it is easier to understand why HPDs will go to extreme lengths to impress others and secure their approval. If they can achieve these goals through being extraordinarily gracious and regal in their personal bearing, they are content. If these tactics fail, temper tantrums of Armageddon proportions will certainly bring them the self-focus they crave, proving the old proverb that negative attention is better than none. Everything about the HPD screams, "Look at me!"

For all their flamboyance and excessively gushing manner of speech, HPDs are very superficial and disingenuous. Looking past their outward, attention-seeking behavior, there is little substance to their personalities. Consider this example, in response to the question, "Tell me about your late father."

Non-HPD: "My dad was remarkable. He was born and raised in rural Oklahoma during the oilfield boom in the Great Depression years. This is where he met my mom, who was the love of his life. When World War II broke out, Dad enlisted in the Army Air Corps, became a pilot, and was commissioned as an officer. Stationed in India, Dad flew 96 missions over the Himalayas, always bringing his crew safely back to base. Then he went to law school on the GI bill and became one of Oklahoma's most successful and prominent attorneys. Personally, Dad was clever, very likeable, completely ethical, and very, very funny! He loved us unconditionally; that was probably his greatest strength — he took people as he found them. When he died, he was still that boy from rural Oklahoma as well as a loving husband, father, and top-notch litigator. I loved him dearly for the example and role model he provided for us."

Histrionic PD: "Oh, Father was just the most wonderful person! Everybody liked him and he was devoted to his family. I've never met anyone quite like Father; God must have broken the mold when he was born. I was his favorite, you know. I could tell by the way he spared no expense to make sure I had everything I wanted. The best schools, the nicest clothes, that sort of thing. I just adored Father and I miss him so terribly. Please excuse my tears, but thinking about my life without Father still wounds me deeply. When he died, I felt like dying too."

Most people scatter when an HPD individual really gets going. HPD women tend to be seductive and flirtatious, calling attention to themselves by their provocative manner of dress and speech. HPD men tend to be hyper-masculine in physical appearance and behavior. With their flashy clothes and romantic seduction, they are accomplished "ladies' men," yet like their female counterparts, they bring no genuine substance to a relationship. HPDs of both genders are vivacious, tempestuous, and have an outward veneer of enchanting sociability. On the flip side, an HPD who is alarmed about perhaps being rejected can do a very fast turnaround into a child-like, clingy, demanding, and emotionally draining person.

CASE STUDY: TYLER

"I'm a corrections officer supervisor in a maximum security prison for men, most of whom are violent offenders, hard-core 'lifers.' It's a tough life, and our primary job is the protection of the public by keeping these offenders incarcerated. These guys are bad to the bone, and I would never turn my back on any of them.

"In corrections, half our time is spent keeping the inmates safe from each other; gang fights, sexual assaults, violence toward staff, you name it and it happens here."

CASE STUDY: TYLER

Tyler was a 42-year-old senior corrections officer with 15 years on the job. He took his responsibilities seriously and was exceptionally concerned about the safety of the prison staff members. "Then one day we got a new commissary clerk. I thought she was some inmate's hot-stuff visitor when I first saw her. When I saw her staff ID tag, I knew right then that my life had just become a whole lot more difficult. She was early thirty-something, long silver-blonde hair, perfect makeup and jewelry, and a figure that would draw any man's eye, much less a bunch of inmates who hadn't seen anything like her in 20 years. She had on a really short skirt, tight blouse, and three-inch spiked heels. Why the hell didn't somebody talk to her about the dress code? She wasn't dressed for working in a men's prison; she looked like she should be on the stroll downtown. I watched her flirt with the inmates and actually felt sorry for them. She had them in the palm of her hand. She wanted attention, and she got it. Me, I was really mad. The commissary is a more open area than the cell blocks, and whenever she was working I had to take three COs off their regular details and put them in the commissary so Miss Short Skirt wouldn't end up being some inmate's baby doll. She looked like she worked at Hooters, not a max-security men's prison. Not only did her performances put her own life in danger, but she put my COs in danger along with her, and I won't tolerate that. She lasted three weeks."

"You had to be a big shot, didn't you, you had to open up your mouth;
You had to have the white hot spotlight,
Front page, bold type…
You had to be a big shot last night."
— Billy Joel
"Big Shot" (paraphrased)

What to Expect From the Histrionic Boss

Employees coping with HPD bosses are often puzzled by how these individuals ever rose to supervisory capacities, given their lack of emotional control and mercurial moods. These bosses attain their positions through natural charm, wit, intelligence, and industrious work performance, winning the confidence of uninformed higher-ups. This is a recipe for disaster for subordinate employees.

HPD bosses are emotional bullies; they are demanding, unpredictable, and barrage an employee with a fast and furious flurry of ideas and problem-solving answers, but they are not the ones who are stuck with untangling this mish-mash and getting a job done. A targeted employee that annoys an HPD boss finds himself berated for not completing a task quickly and accurately; in reality, this bully is so difficult to communicate with, it is often impossible to sort out what he or she wants done, when the task is due, and what the task must entail. Because these bosses are so unorganized and superficial, they blame the target for being confounded by what is expected of him or her with no insight into their own impossible management style.

A target of the histrionic, or several targets, notes that the boss flits around the office or section with seemingly crucial purpose; in reality the boss has only superficial and dramatic purposes that are seriously lacking in actual purpose. This bully makes a mess of things and then attacks the target with melodramatic and exaggerated ire for failing to clean up the mess. The target of an HPD boss is inadvertently selected as such due to his or her lack of tolerance and understanding of the boss's bullying behavior. It takes a very thick skin to survive the bullying of an HPD boss, not taking the bullying too seriously or personally. Still, targets of these bosses tend to have a short lifespan on the job and burn out quickly due to sheer emotional exhaustion from being singled out for the bully's negative, critical workplace dramas.

What to Expect From the Histrionic Coworker

Working with an HPD coworker can be both entertaining and tiresome. She knows all the office gossip and never fails to embellish it as she passes it along; amusing unless a particular employee ends up as the target of this type of bullying. Dramatic gossip and rumors are the main weapons in this bully's arsenal. He dishes the dirt on the target to maintain superiority and attention among workplace coworkers. Other employees rarely realize that this is a form of bullying; they assume it is just harmless histrionics that harms no one.

HPD coworkers are especially adept at recruiting others to take their side against the target; their convincing charisma lures other coworkers into believing that the bully really does know things about the target that they do not know. Both male and female HPD bullies use their seductive demeanor to entice others into mob bullying the bewildered target. Other coworkers can easily get caught up in the HPD bully's emotional chaos that, supposedly, is caused and/or perpetuated by the target. If an HPD bully is unable to attain attention and admiration from a coworker, he or she will roar into so many fits of temper and distress that the target would willingly transfer to Katmandu just to get away from the daily endurance contests.

The HPD bullying coworker is especially flamboyant when he or she is pursuing a raise or promotion. To achieve this goal, the bully must make everyone else seem lackluster in work performance compared to him. His charming charisma helps him sell himself to the higher-ups, while the honest and reliable target(s) appear mediocre in comparison.

What to Expect From the Histrionic Subordinate

As the manager of an HPD subordinate, one's patience and discernment abilities will be put to the test daily. This subordinate can come across as a manager's most ardent supporter or worst enemy, sometimes running this gamut within a single work day. The HPD subordinate's manner of bullying is covert, compared to an HPD boss's overt, attention-seeking behavior. The HPD subordinate bully gets her way by constantly needing attention and approval from the manager. If she fails to get it, she will plunge the workplace into melodrama by pouting, crying at her desk where others are sure to see her, throwing temper tantrums in the break room, and otherwise disrupting the flow of doing business. The weary manager quickly learns to lavish praise upon this bully, even if it is mostly undeserved, just to keep him from plunging the work day into trauma. This is an unwinnable situation for the manager of an HPD bullying subordinate; the higher-ups want productivity, not excuses about histrionic, unmanageable subordinates. To maintain productivity, the manager is bullied into keeping the office at peace by smoothing the HPD subordinate's need for admiration and praise.

"What we have here is a failure to communicate."
—From the movie *Cool Hand Luke*

The HPD bullying subordinate is quick with ideas, and slow on follow-through. She takes public credit for being the impetus of innovative ideas, but it is her long-suffering manager who must put these truly good ideas into practice. The bully knows this; all she has to do is appear witty and creative in public, and then drop the ball into the target manager's lap. The vicious circle is completed when a higher-up who liked the HPD subordinate's idea completes the necessary follow-through.

Practical work-related matters are foreign to HPD bullying subordinates. Since everything in their personal and professional lives is a crisis, they will not think twice about bullying the manager into giving them the day off — with pay — because of a personal crisis. Only a heartless manager would deny this request, or so will say the bully to coworkers when his or her request is indeed denied.

The Borderline

Although the DSM-IV-TR concisely explains the characteristics of the Borderline Personality Disorder (BPD), it does not explain where the disorder got its name. Nonclinicians and new mental health students are also puzzled by this. To explain, this personality disorder's name is derived from its observed behavior that demonstrates a fine line between mental health stability and psychotic states. The world of the borderline is like walking a tightrope; stability is difficult to maintain. Fall to one side, and all will be well. Fall to the other side and emotional and behavior chaos erupts, sometimes to the extent of partial or full-blown psychosis. The borderline is much more emotionally volatile than even the histrionic; moods are more extreme and unpredictable, and irrational beliefs can become psychotically delusional. Of all the personality disorders, the BPD is the most difficult for clinicians to treat; the presence in the workplace ranges from mildly annoying to unbearable for the entire organization from the top to the bottom of the employee chain. If the Histrionic Personality Disorder is disruptive, the borderline is sheer devastation in a work environment.

The DSM-IV-TR defines the Borderline Personality Disorder as follows:

- A pervasive pattern of instability in interpersonal relationships, self-image and moods, and chronic impulsivity

- Frantic efforts to avoid real or imagined abandonment

- A pattern of unstable and intense interpersonal relationships characterized by alternating extremes of idealization and devaluation

- Identity disturbance marked by persistently unstable self-image

- Impulsivity in areas that are potentially self-damaging

- Recurrent suicidal behavior, gestures, or threats; self-mutilating behavior

- Mood instability, e.g., depression, irritability, or anxiety rarely lasting more than a few days

- Chronic feelings of emotional emptiness

- Inappropriate, intense anger or difficulty controlling anger

- Transient, stress-related paranoid ideation or severe dissociative symptoms

"Good employers purge bullies;
Bad ones promote them."

This list clearly differentiates between the Histrionic Personality Disorder and the Borderline Personality Disorder, but an example will help the nonclinician fully understand the characteristics of the BPD in the workplace.

CASE STUDY: JACKSON

"I'm a security police sergeant," Jackson told his military mental health therapist. "Four months ago I was assigned a new partner, a female senior airman who just transferred in. Since I supervised her, I reviewed her performance reports and saw that although she was smart, well-trained, and energetic on the job, she had trouble getting along with people both in her dorm and on the job. She went through three partners in only a month.

"I thought it would be best if she rode with me on patrol so I could see what the problem was. Everything was good at first. Angelina was really nice, talkative, and cheerful. I found out that she won a marksmanship medal in security police training, both on the 9mm and the semiautomatic rifle. Pretty good; better than I ever did.

"One night we responded to a domestic disturbance on base and Angelina took the lead. She separated the spouses, calmed everybody down, and restored order. Her written report was perfect. Then day by day, the problems started. Angelina had these weird moods that changed in a split second. I never knew when she would be cheerful, then angry, then crying about some damn thing. It was crazy.

"I verbally counseled her one day when she got mad and threw a full coffee cup onto the wall during guard mount (beginning of shift). Then she decided she hated me. First, I was her mentor, and then she hated me. Go figure.

"What really scared me is the morning in physical training when she had on a sleeveless tank top and shorts and I saw what looked like cut marks on her upper arms and thighs. I asked her about them and she acted like it was no big deal, that she'd accidentally run into some wire. That's not what it looked like to me.

"The entire squadron was afraid of her. Either you were her best friend or you were the Antichrist. You were on a pedestal or you were crap. Angelina was always extreme; there was no middle ground with her. I kept her riding

CASE STUDY: JACKSON

with me, but by the time our shift was over, I was just plain exhausted from her moods, her blaming, devotion to people she barely knew, crying, and her temper.

"It all came to a head when she got a DUI off base. Her mental health evaluation said that she was a binge drinker. She couldn't drive on base for a year and couldn't carry a weapon. She couldn't be deployed. In other words, she was useless to us. I put her on dispatch duty and initiated involuntary separation action. Angelina just went wild. She started talking all this paranoid stuff about people in the squadron, including the Commander, being out to get her. She couldn't control herself. She'd scream about how much she hated the military one minute, and the next minute she was threatening to kill herself if she lost her career. I told her mental health provider about those cut marks I saw on her. Then she decided that people in the squadron were following her, and that did it.

"She went to a psych hospital until she was finally discharged. I guess I blame myself a little bit because I couldn't help her with her problems, but I'm also glad she isn't here anymore."

"I changed jobs after 13 years rather than deal with her any longer. I couldn't treat everyone equally because she always put me in positions where I had to give her her own way or have the office in constant turmoil and complaints filed against me. My other workers kept asking me to do something about her; when I tried, she made sure it backfired on me by throwing a fit. She just wore me down."

—Manager of an BPD subordinate

Jackson experienced the full brunt of the Borderline Personality Disorder in the workplace, the greatest challenge to supervisors and coworkers. Any organization must run smoothly, cooperatively, and efficiently in order to prosper; the BPD's core problem is a complete inability to form and maintain stable interpersonal relationships. Their explosive, out-of-control tempers cause them to lash out wildly at anyone around them, caring little about who they damage. Living or working with a BPD is like riding a roller coaster with its extreme highs and lows coming at a furious, fast pace. "I hate your guts! Please do not leave me!" is the borderline's anthem. Borderlines have no "gray areas"; they live in extremes. Highly intense and stormy interpersonal relationships mark the home and workplace with a BPD in residence.

The most alarming behaviors of the BPD are suicide attempts and self-mutilation. Jackson noted the cut marks on Angelina's arms and thighs; BPDs are the only personality disorders known for "cutting." Since they have such a tornado of internal emotions, cutting is their way of putting their pain on the outside instead of feeling inside. Cutting is not a suicidal gesture; when BPDs make one of their frequent suicide gestures or attempts, they make their intentions quite clear. In the workplace, employees are very alarmed when they see scars or fresh cutting marks.

What to Expect From the Borderline Boss

In discussing "volatile managers," Dr. Roy Lubit wrote that these bosses have short fuses that burn with remarkable speed, especially when they are under stress. Subordinates who catch them on the wrong day or at the wrong time find themselves facing a deluge or anger about trivial issues. The astonished employee feels as if the boss was just waiting for someone to scream at, and he or she was unfortunate enough to become the target of all that negative emotion. Employees of a borderline boss are constantly on guard and ill at ease.

The BPD boss is a consummate bully. Since he has no concept of limits or boundaries, he bullies subordinates by intruding upon their thoughts, feelings, and personal lives, and then twisting this information into negative feedback and gossip. A targeted employee becomes, at some times, the boss's favorite, and at other times, the problem child of the work section. The targeted employee has no idea which she will be from day to day. She will receive public high praise on Monday, and then public criticism on Thursday for no discernable reason.

Borderline bosses are like an empty bucket with a hole in it; no matter how much sand an employee pours into the bucket, it remains empty. This sense of internal emptiness is characteristic of the BPD. While a targeted employee reassures the BPD boss that he is loyal and devoted, this bully still feels that pervasive emptiness and will fly into a rage when there is a threat to the relationship between the bullying boss and the targeted employee. Employees constantly walk on eggshells for fear of setting off the BPD boss's volatile moods. These bosses bully by vacillating between idealizing and then devaluating employees. Harshly criticized, a targeted employee is befuddled when he is highly praised in his performance report. BPDs bully through unpredictability; employees find themselves keeping peace at any price regardless of what their own good judgment tells them. Bullying borderline bosses are also adept at drawing others into their workplace drama, setting one employee against another; woe to the employee who opposes the BPD boss. Fear of rejection and abandonment by an employee is intolerable to this bully.

A workplace dominated by a bullying BPD boss is an unhappy workplace. Employees lie low, keep their heads down, and concentrate on their tasks without the benefit of pleasant camaraderie with other coworkers. The fear and anxiety level in the workplace is always high, contributing to an overall atmosphere of intense stress. Employees wonder what mood the boss will be in when he writes their performance report; will the boss praise them or devalue them? Employees feel helpless in steering their own careers due to the volatility of the boss.

The most puzzling feature of the BPD boss is that, in most cases, his or her bullying is not intentional as it is with other personality disordered bosses. As the snake said to the frog in the fable cited earlier, "It's my nature."

What to Expect From the Borderline Coworker

"For the borderline, feelings are facts."
—Cavaiola & Lavender

Expect to be misunderstood. Expect that a BPD coworker will have personal agendas that are played out in the workplace. Expect that BPD coworkers will fear rejection, and then behave in manners that actually invite rejection. Expect professional boundaries to be continually breeched. Marital problems, incorrigible kids, abusive boyfriends/girlfriends, etc. will be on full, uncomfortable display for all to hear. The BPD coworker bullies others by demanding their full attention to his or her personal chaos. If this attention is not given, this bully will add the offending coworkers to the list of people who have rejected him or her.

In many ways, the BPD employee comes to work each day for two reasons: first, to earn a living, and second, to entangle others into her personal and professional drama. Like huge whirlpools, BPD coworkers attempt to suck others into the chaos of their ever-changing emotions. Life without drama, to them, is no life at all. These bullying coworkers will ask others to lie for them about their absenteeism, cover for them when they are too distraught to work, and bend the rules for them when they take three-hour lunch breaks. The coworker who refuses to engage in the BPD's dramatics will be bullied unmercifully by constant barrages about his unsympathetic character, her disloyalty, and his despicable refusal to join the BPD in workplace chaos.

CASE STUDY: JASON

Jason was a 33-year-old employee of a business that provided office furniture to local companies. He worked for the business for five years and had an excellent work record. Recently, the business hired Caroline as a bookkeeper for the business; Jason and Caroline often worked together when making estimates of the costs of office furniture to local companies.

"I liked Caroline right away," Jason stated. "She was cheerful, energetic, and a little bit sexy. I enjoyed working with her because she was really good at putting together furniture bids for local companies. Then one day I came to work and couldn't help noticing that Caroline was crying at her desk, which was across from mine. I asked her if she was okay and what was wrong. She replied that her boyfriend had hit her last night, and that this was not the first time this had happened. I postponed my work tasks to talk with her in the break room for a while. She seemed okay, and we all went on with our work. Two days later, Caroline told me that our section manager counseled her about bringing her personal problems to work. She was really upset about this. How could our boss be so unsympathetic? I felt like taking her side. A few days later, she told me that her boyfriend had been unfaithful to her, and I felt like comforting her. Our boss called me in and talked to me about not getting involved in Caroline's personal problems. I didn't tell Caroline about this, but I became less willing to talk with her about her problems with the boyfriend. Caroline didn't take this well. She accused me of siding with her boyfriend, who I didn't even know, and being disloyal to her. I just wanted to do my work, and I wanted Caroline to just do her work and leave me out of her personal life. It was too much for me. Before I knew it, Caroline hated me and told all our coworkers that I was just a 'male chauvinist pig' who sided with her boyfriend. I didn't even know him! She was always either crying at work or she was having angry tirades about men in general. What was I supposed to do? I couldn't do my work and deal with Caroline's problems at the same time."

What to Expect From the Borderline Subordinate

Initially, managers of BPD subordinates regard these employees as too good to be true. They are optimistic, charming, energetic and creative; everything a boss needs to put a gold star on his or her section. After a few weeks of hiring these individuals, the manager begins to suspect the terrible truth; this star employee is an emotional and behavioral mess, dragging the workplace into his or her chaotic thoughts and feelings. This subordinate bullies and dominates the workplace through luring others, including the manager, into his internal turmoil that takes center stage instead of crucial work tasks. The manager of a BPD subordinate wonders what happened to her calm, productive work environment since the new employee arrived. To restore order to the workplace, the manager feels compelled to help this bullying employee solve his personal problems just to resume the unit's productiveness.

> *"Think of the Glenn Close character in the movie* Fatal Attraction. *That character epitomizes the borderline personality. One minute she is seductive and alluring, but as soon as there are hints of the affair ending, she slits her wrists in a wild frenzy of hatred."*
> **— Cavaiola & Lavender**

Like other personality disorders, the BPD subordinate bullies bosses and coworkers through a complex behavioral history of bringing personal dramas into the workplace as well as inciting drama in the workplace itself. When the BPD employee senses that his or her coworkers have reached their limit, he or she upgrades issues to the manager. According to this bully, coworkers are cruel and unsympathetic. She complains that the workplace is unbearably inhumane. He expresses concern about rejection and isolation from other subordinates. The litany of rejection and disloyalty is endless; the manager is at a loss about how to restore order and productivity to the workplace.

Managers of a BPD subordinate should expect moodiness, absenteeism for personal reasons, separation of coworkers into "us" versus "them," and staff splitting between sympathetic and unsympathetic coworkers. While terminating the toxic borderline is always an alternative, these employees are known for their litigious nature. They bully their way into keeping their jobs through threats of lawsuits; unlike the narcissistic or histrionic subordinate, the borderline employee often follows through with these threats.

Managing the BPD employee takes patience and precise documentation of this subordinate's actions if termination action is pursued. Managers must keep in mind that personality disorders are managed, but not cured. Their best hope is to refer these subordinates to counseling services to create a higher functioning borderline.

The Obsessive-Compulsive

These individuals are more interested in telling employees what they know than what others think. They are not interested in sharing ideas, but are very interested in the faults of others. Interpersonal relationships are unimportant; only perfectionism and a total focus on completing tasks matters. Emotional propriety is meaningless and unknown territory. Decision-making in the workplace is based upon logic and rational principles, not upon what is popular among other employees. The obsessive-compulsive employee is rigid, resistant to new ideas, suspicious of others, and cannot tolerate anything less than imperfect performance by himself and other employees. There is a "right" way and a "wrong" way to complete a task; their way is the only acceptable way.

The DSM-IV-TR describes the Obsessive-Compulsive Personality Disorder (OCPD) as follows:

- A pervasive pattern of perfectionism and inflexibility

- Perfectionism that interferes with task completion

- Preoccupation with details, rules, lists, order, organization, and schedules to the point where the major point of the task is lost

- Unreasonable insistence that others submit to his or her easy way of doing things because of the conviction that others will not do them correctly

- Excessive devotion to work and productivity to the exclusion of leisure activities and friendships

- Indecisiveness; decision-making is either avoided, postponed, or protracted

- Over-conscientiousness, scrupulousness, and inflexibility about matters of morality, ethics, or values

- Lack of generosity in giving time, money, or gifts when no personal gain is likely to result

- Restricted expression of moods

- Inability to discard worn-out or worthless object even when they have no sentimental value. A distinction must be drawn between the Obsessive-Compulsive Personality Disorder and the Obsessive-Compulsive Disorder (OCD).

As previously mentioned, personality disorders reflect patterns of personal characteristics and behaviors; they are not mental illnesses, and they cannot be "cured" or put into remission through therapy and medication. The Obsessive-Compulsive Disorder is a mental illness that is characterized by continuous thoughts (obsessions) and actions (compulsions) that the sufferer is unable to stop; these thoughts and actions are on an endless loop in the sufferer's mind. For example, an employee cannot stop thinking about the soup he spilled in the break room's microwave, so he spends hours cleaning the microwave over and over, and checking constantly to make sure no one else has spilled something in it. OCD is caused by faulty chemicals in the brain and can be well controlled with medication. OCPD has some characteristics in common with OCD, but a personality disorder is not a chemically induced brain disorder. Having an OCPD in the workplace as a manager, coworker, or subordinate has a significant impact on other employees. This personality style affects how he interacts with others, what he wants from others, and what might lead him to become angry with others. OCPDs have an odd and troublesome style of perception, i.e., how they view themselves, others, and circumstances or situations.

"People who know the least seem to know it the loudest."
— Author

The reality of the OCPD's perception is focused entirely upon details; they are unable to see the "big picture" as illustrated by the saying that someone cannot see the forest, only the trees. They have great difficulty determining which details are important and which are trivial. Due to this excessive focus on details, OCPDs are very critical of people and tasks that are less than perfect. Adrift in a sea of details, they have difficulty making concrete, final decisions; there is always a "But what about..." in their attempts to make a decision and stick with it. While the OCPD is lost in meticulous (and often meaningless) details, tasks remain incomplete and deadlines are missed. Still, they are unable to see any value in the perceptions of others.

OCPDs work single-mindedly and deny themselves days off and other types of relaxation and recreation. In the workplace, they are first in and last out, working compulsively to prove to themselves and others that they are competent, valuable employees. Their pervasive fear of appearing to be less than perfect makes them anxious, overly serious, and very tense. Even when they burn out by keeping up this impossible pace on the job, they believe that working even harder and longer will somehow magically restore them to their pre-burnout stage. This irrational and unrealistic perception is played out in the workplace among managers, coworkers, and subordinates, creating a stressful and frustration work environment.

"There is no 'reality,' only perception."
— Dr. P. C. McGraw

What to Expect From the Obsessive-Compulsive Boss

"My way or the highway" is a good summation of what employees can expect from the OCPD manager. Long on minutia and short on personal warmth, the OCPD boss bullies others through his or her rigid expectations on how tasks must be performed. This workplace bully is not interested in the ideas or opinions of others; an employee who dares to offer a new, faster and better way of completing a task will be targeted by the OCPD boss because they perceive the target as a disrespectful, upstart troublemaker. Once such an employee becomes the target of this type of bullying boss, she can expect to retain that label indefinitely; she will be unable to redeem herself in the boss's eyes even if she figures out this bully's personality style and tries to lie low and stay quiet. So rigid is the OCPDs thought pattern, changes are unbearable and impossible. This bullying boss will form a negative perception of an employee that never changes despite the target's success with tasks. Criticism comes easily to the OCPD boss, but praise, compliments, raises, and bonuses are nonexistent. Targets of this type of bullying feel harassed, unappreciated, and devalued because they *are*.

The OCPD bullying boss, overwhelmed by trivial details, may be the least informed person in the office, yet she will loudly and vehemently proclaim that her way of doing things is the only correct way. Besieged targets will shake their heads in frustration and then do as they are told rather than face a tirade about their incompetence and failure to follow instructions.

Since this bully works compulsively through long hours, as well as on weekends and holidays, he expects his subordinates to do the same. The boss will not see this as bullying, but as a good work ethic; those employees who resist being bullied through compulsive workloads will be viewed as lazy, lacking motivation, and disinterested in the greater good of the company.

Another bullying tactic of the OCPD boss is excessive micromanagement. Since his way is the only way, employees can expect the boss to constantly check to make sure tasks are being done "right." A subordinate who successfully completes a task by a manner that is "wrong" will be required to repeat the task the boss's way, achieving the same results. For this bullying boss, a task is not complete unless it is done his way.

Somber, tense, and inflexible are terms that describe the workplace with an OCPD bullying boss. Employees should not expect Christmas parties, "Get well soon" cards, birthday cakes, or Saturday group golf games. No one is going to receive a gift certificate from the boss for being Employee of the Month. Instead, employees will be bullied through impossible tasks, short deadlines, long hours, micromanagement, impersonal treatment, being bogged down in trivial details, demands of perfection, and hypercritical harassment.

What to Expect From the Obsessive-Compulsive Coworker

Cavaiola and Lavender describe OCPD coworkers as either a blessing or a curse, depending upon their level of functioning and willingness to be a team player. An emotionally secure OCPD coworker who wants to fit in with the office group will not cause much of a problem except through his nitpicking and overattention to details. When the other employees have had enough, he will respond well when told to "take a chill pill."

Employees who are cursed with an insecure and impersonal OCPD coworker must watch each others' backs. This coworker will bully others by creating a "me versus them" atmosphere in the workplace, using fairly sophisticated spy techniques to detect and record the errors of others, and sharing negative information about other employees with the boss. Being sticklers for rules, the OCPD coworker bullies by constantly pointing out rule violations to others, even the minutest errors like writing a phone message on a sheet of paper rather than the message forms. "You are not supposed to…" is this bully's favorite phrase when it comes to rules and policies.

The OCPD coworker is envious of another's success and will sabotage it if he can, not out of meanness or spite, but because he does not believe your work merits a bonus, raise, or promotion. Constantly critical, lacking in self-esteem, and mired in indecisiveness, this bully will be threatened by a coworker's success and will let the entire office know that the success was due to her efforts, not her subordinate.

CASE STUDY: TERRY

Terry was a 25-year-old law student who went to school at night and worked for a judge in the probate court as a deputy court clerk during the day. His coworker, Zach, was in his late 60s and worked as the judge's bailiff. It was well known in the probate division that Zach did not care for young law students; he found them irresponsible, believed they had poor work ethics, they did not adhere to office rules, and performed their jobs incorrectly.

"This old geezer is on me constantly, telling me what to do and how to do it," Terry told his academic adviser. "Our judge is a great guy; he always lets law students study after they finish their work or when we're waiting for a jury to reach a verdict. This makes Zach crazy; he thinks everybody should be working all the time like he does. If he doesn't have any real work to do, he'll make some up just to be doing something. Even the judge plays cards with a bunch of clerks during our lunch break; Zach just keeps working. Plus, he's got the personality of a dead fish."

"I invited him to my wedding and of course he didn't bother to show up. Everybody but Zach signed a 'congratulations' card for us. He's so uptight, he told me that couples shouldn't live together before they're married; I told him my personal life was none of his damn business. Zach wrote up this weird schedule about who takes breaks at what time and the order in which work should be done. He's not in charge of the office, but he had every minute of the day listed and accounted for. Nobody even paid attention to him.

"I have to pass his desk to get to the judge's chambers, and once I

CASE STUDY: TERRY

noticed that his calendar was filled with a bunch of notes in shorthand.

"Zach had no idea that I can read shorthand. The notes were all about me; dates where I was five minutes late for work, when I used the phone for a personal call, when I was studying for an exam in the break room, little nitpicky things. One time we were waiting for a jury to come in and I was about to be late for class. I told the judge that I'd call my professor and explain why I missed class. But Zach said no, he'd stay, I should go on to class.

"The judge thought he was just being nice, but the real reason he wanted to stay is because he practically lives at the office; it's his whole life. When I first started working there I asked him out to lunch — my treat. He said no thanks; he brought his own lunch every day. He eats in the file room; God forbid he should have to make conversation with somebody.

"I know I'm a day late in turning in this paper, but I had a problem with Zach about it. Yesterday the judge was still on vacation so there was no court. I planned to finish my paper at work on my computer since my laptop is broken. Zach had a fit, saying that there are rules about not using work computers for personal reasons. I wasn't bothering anyone and I know the judge wouldn't have minded. But Zach made such a stink about it, I just gave it up and borrowed my friend's laptop. Then Zach advised me that we're not supposed to do personal work in the office. I was so angry by then, I called the chief court clerk and asked for the afternoon off to finish my paper. That was fine, but my friend needed his laptop back, so I didn't have my paper finished last night, but I finished it today whether Zach liked it or not."

What to Expect From the Obsessive-Compulsive Subordinate

According to Cavaiola and Lavender, renowned Freudian analyst and author Karen Horney (1950) wrote that individuals with OCPD are governed by "the tyranny of the should." How people should act, think, and feel, tasks should be accomplished, everything should be structured, and rules should be established and enforced. The OCPD subordinate will wonder, "Why is Ted the boss? Molly's smarter and does things the right way; Molly should be the boss." What this subordinate does not understand is that although Mr. Spock was the most intelligent crew member of the Enterprise, it was Capt. Kirk's leadership abilities that put him in command. The OCPD subordinate bullies through undermining the boss and other employees by unduly criticizing the work of others, filing complaints about policy violations, insisting on having her own way, and creating a competitive atmosphere among the other employees about who works the hardest. She is certain to win this competition since she comes in early, stays late, takes work home, and works on weekends. Again, she makes a thinking error; workplaces are not about who works the hardest, but who works the best; who consistently produces top-quality work for the company that is completed on time and advances the mission of the company. The manager of an OCPD subordinate will find that he needs a great deal of supervision to keep him from being sidetracked by bullying others and getting lost in the trivial details of a task. Since coworkers often come to the manager for relief from being bullied, this bully is not difficult to spot. He too will frequently appear in the manager's office with tales of tasks not being done correctly and rules that are being broken. Going to the boss is merely another bullying tactic since the OCPD subordinate makes sure that his target knows he is complaining once again about him or her.

"I asked my subordinate to plan the date, time, and agenda for our monthly staff meeting. He scheduled the meeting for September 11th, the first year after the terrorist attacks. Many staff members had already made plans to attend memorial services and events, and so had I. A senior staff member told me that my subordinate told them that the meeting was mandatory and if they cared about the company's success, they'd better change their plans because it's against the rules to take time off instead of attending

important meetings. Then I looked at the agenda he'd drawn up for this 'important meeting.' It was all silly trivia like whose turn it was to fill the water cooler and not taking the phone book out of the front office. What all this had to do with the company's success, I can't imagine."

—Manager of an OCPD subordinate

The Dependant

"Did you hear the one about the dependant who fell off a cliff? Someone else's life passed in front of his eyes!"
— Cavaiola & Lavender

In the workplace, individuals with the Dependent Personality Disorder (DPD) give value to everyone's opinion but their own. Sigmund Freud first identified these personality features almost a century ago. He noted that dependent features are found more in women than men, that they are "clingy" and excessively needy and accommodating to others, and they are distinctly over-involved in the lives of others because they fear being rejected and alone. In other words, people with dependent personalities have little self-identity since their values, morals, beliefs and actions are all geared toward pleasing others. They frequently endure a lot of verbal and physical abuse — including bullying in the workplace — rather than leave a problematic life situation when it is clearly in their best interest to leave. They are a bully's perfect target; they take whatever is dished out to them without complaint.

The DSM-IV-TR contains these features of the Dependant Personality Disorder:

- A pervasive, excessive need to be taken care of, leading to submissive and clinging behavior and fear of separation

- Difficulty making decisions without excessive amounts of advice and reassurance from others

- Difficulty disagreeing with others out of fear of rejection and the need for approval

- Inability initiating projects or doing things alone due to poor self-confidence

- Goes to excessive lengths to obtain nurturance and support from others; often volunteers for unpleasant duties

- Feelings of discomfort and helplessness if alone; exaggerated fears of being unable to care for themselves

- Urgently seeks another relationship as a source of care and support when another relationship ends

- Unrealistic preoccupation with fears of being left alone to care for themselves

Having a DPD in the workplace feels quite like being smothered in plastic wrap: unable to make a move without this excessively needy individual latched onto you like a leech that slowly and steadily bleeds you dry. There is no escape from the DPD; they are at everyone's desk or in everyone's office seeking constant advice, reassurance, and approval. They have very poor assertiveness skills, finding it impossible to disagree with anyone, mumbling instead of speaking clearly, deferring to the opinions and decisions of others, and have difficulty maintaining eye contact. Their body language strongly speaks of their lack of self-assurance and they tend to dismiss or underplay their accomplishments.

The DPD sees "powerful" and "competent" employers and employees as essential to their survival in the workplace. Without clinging to these people, the DPD feels devoid of sustenance, weak and helpless to initiate or achieve anything on their own. They tend to over-idealize others whom they see as powerful while refusing to acknowledge that all people have faults and shortcomings. The DPD often has an irrational belief that there is some kind of special bond between them and their powerful workplace idols.

It seems unlikely that the DPD employer, coworker, or subordinate is capable of bullying others, yet they do so continually. Instead of narcissistic or antisocial aggression, the DPD bullies others in their workplace by different means such as inflicting feelings of guilt for being impatient with or rejecting the afflicted employee, making it widely known in the workplace that the object of their idolization disapproves of or dislikes them, appearing emotionally devastated when told to "Please let me get on with my own work and figure this out for yourself," and becoming immobile and incapable of initiating projects and making decisions. The DPD individual bullies others by being a pest, and a pitiful pest at that. Others find themselves giving in to the DPD's peculiar bullying tactics simply to placate them and hope they will go away.

What to Expect From the Dependent Personality Disorder Boss

Employees often wonder how the excessively needy DPD bosses get promoted in the first place. Normally, they make better followers than leaders. If these individuals have succeeded in advancing into a management position, it is usually because they go to great lengths to please their own bosses, not because they have a particular affinity for competition and advancement.

In the workplace, the DPD boss will avoid disharmony and confrontation; he or she wants to please everyone all of the time. Thus, these individuals may achieve a lower level of management but rarely make it to the "top" of their organization.

> **Coworker:** Please call Mr. Jones for me. He's really angry with us, and I know I'll just mess it up.
>
> **You:** I have my own work to do. Can't you take care of this yourself?
>
> **Coworker:** I'll just make it worse. Please, can you help me?

The DPD boss will stridently attempt to create a disharmony-free workplace. Fearful and uncertain about making decisions, this boss will bully others into making decisions through manifestation of his or her uncertainty and vulnerability. An employee will find himself making decisions, rather than the boss. The targeted employee will grow weary, angry, and frustrated at having to do the boss's job, especially if the subordinate has made a woeful decision that backfired. Instead of taking the proverbial bull by the horns and making a decision — unpopular or not — this bully will leave it to a subordinate to take the heat of making a difficult decision. Once the DPD boss zeroes in on a target subordinate that will do this, she will abdicate responsibility in the workplace and bully her way into making a subordinate take the fall of office decisions.

The DPD boss has difficulty functioning individually on the job. Finding a target employee, this bully will rely completely on a subordinate's ideas and opinions. To avoid endless discussions on "what should I do" with the boss, the target employee, weary and frustrated, will say anything, agree with anything, just to get this subtly bullying boss out of the way. In these cases, the efficiency of the workplace is seriously compromised. Talk, talk, and even more talk do not forward the goals of the workplace.

What to Expect From the Dependent Coworker

"Help me!" is the anthem of the DPD coworker. "Do my job, which I'm scared to do because it might create disharmony." This bully does not impose himself by force, like narcissists and antisocial coworkers do; on the contrary, this coworker bullies by helplessness. The targeted employee is competent and self-assured; qualities the DPD coworker lacks. Instead of being rewarded for his or her competence, the targeted employee is engaged in a parasitic relationship with the DPS coworker.

The target of this bully feels merciful toward the incompetent and needy fellow worker, and has no idea that he or she is being bullied into doing a job that is not his or her responsibility. Targets feel sorry for their bullies, not realizing how they are being used and bullied. The DPD coworkers constantly seek rescue from making decisions and coping with potential disharmony with the business's clients. By their stated vulnerability, they bully others into doing their jobs for them. Their fears of rejection and abandonment take center stage, regardless of how this affects targeted coworkers. DPD coworkers can appear quite sincere and pitiful in their pleas for help; it is very difficult for a coworker to understand that he or she is actually being bullied into doing things that the DPD coworker should do.

What to Expect From the Dependent Subordinate

A DPS subordinate will never be able to function independently; this is the first thing that employers and supervisors must grasp. While it is possible to mentor these employees to the point where they can be functional in the workplace, they will not be company "go-getters." They require a large amount of reassurance, mentoring, and instructions from their managers. Without this, they will flounder. Do not expect a straightforward answer from the DPD subordinate; their favorite phrase is "Did I do okay?" For the workplace manager, the DPD subordinate bully does so by seeking constant approval and reassurance, taking much time away from the manager's work schedule. This subtle form of workplace bullying may seem only innocuous and annoying, but in fact it creates disruption in the mission of the workplace.

The DPD subordinate's bullying agenda is "take care of me"; security, safety, and acceptance. Instead of simply being fired, this bully has a knack at making other feel sorry for him or her. They are loyal, eager to please, and personally pleasing. It is difficult to fire them since they appear so well-meaning. Yet, the DPD subordinate's bullying tactics will reduce a workplace to ruins through the constant need of advice and approval by any means necessary. They can reduce a productive workplace into a psychological hotbed in an awfully short period of time. Managers can expect excessive sick days, disability claims, resignations, and requests for extended leave days for these fragile employees.

According to Cavaiola and Lavender, DPD subordinates can be removed from a toxic, bullying situation through the use of "graded assignments." This is a favored technique of psychotherapists to assist patients in a step-by-step method of overcoming their personal fears. Through therapeutic means, the DPD subordinate is helped to create a solid, positive sense of self-esteem and a decrease in reliance (e.g. bullying) of others. This is accomplished through assertiveness training and individual therapy to help the DPD patient to become more confident, positive, and a full member of the workplace.

The Schizoid

Ted Kaczynski was a loner, completely devoid of being able to form and maintain interpersonal relationships with others. Although he was mathematically brilliant and a Harvard graduate at age 20, Kaczynski was never able to form social relationships. After achieving his Ph.D. in mathematics, he was an assistant professor at the University of California, Berkeley campus.

Kaczynski resigned from this position because he was not a very good teacher, being unable to relate with students. In 1971, Kaczynski moved to a shack in the mountains near Lincoln, Montana; it had no electricity, plumbing, or running water. He only ventured into Lincoln to purchase small amounts of food with money sent to him by his mother and brother. In the solitude of the Rocky Mountains, Kaczynski began to build and send bombs to those he felt were allowing technology to ruin the ecology of the world. As the "Unabomber," he wrote a lengthy, rambling "manifesto" that he demanded be published in newspapers or he would kill again. His brother recognized his writing style and reported his identity to the FBI so the killings would cease. Ted Kaczynski is now serving life in prison.

Although his case is an extreme example of the Schizoid Personality Disorder (SPD), Kaczynski manifests many schizoid features such as extreme social introversion, an intense need to be left alone, and an emphasis on intellectual skills rather than social skills. Schizoids seem aloof, distant, and cold. In the workplace, they simply do their jobs without becoming involved in any office social friendships or activities. They lack spontaneity and are indifferent to human relationships. While they are often perceived as arrogant, this usually is not the case although they are often quite intelligent. They simply exist in a world of their own and resist intrusion by others. It is interesting to note that the majority of SPDs are male, unmarried Caucasians.

An ASPD is incapable of participating in office chit-chat, sharing lunches, telling stories about their families, and other social workplace interactions. It is important to note that schizoids do not feel that their behavior is unusual or problematic; they are merely indifferent to interpersonal relationships. Thus, they live a life virtually devoid of emotional interactions and do not view this as problematic. Their emotional makeup is flat, lifeless, and devoid of feeling. Their communication style is loose, lacking in focus and direction. Their body language is just as devoid of depth; they speak in monotones, saying as little as possible in a polite but perfunctory, formal manner. When finding themselves in the uncharted (and unwanted) world of emotions, they simply withdraw from the situation.

SPDs prefer to work with inanimate objects like machinery and computers; jobs at which they excel because human contact with others can easily be avoided. Not understanding the rules of workplace social interactions, they may try to imitate the social actions of others but in a very mechanical, emotionless manner that is a mere façade — and not a very good one.

The DSM-IV-TR describes the Schizoid Personality Disorder in this manner:

- A pervasive pattern of detachment from social relationships and a restricted range of expression of emotions in interpersonal settings

- Neither desires nor enjoys close relationships, including being part of a family

- Almost always chooses solitary activities

- Has little, if any, interest in having sexual experiences with another person

- Takes pleasure in few, if any, activities

- Lacks close friends or confidants other than first-degree relatives

- Appears indifferent to the praise or criticism of others

- Shows emotional coldness, detachment, or flattened mood

An SPD can wreak havoc in a workplace; not understanding or caring about the needs of others, being insensitive to verbal and nonverbal clues, unable to comprehend social etiquette, and having no need for contact with others. This is a worker whom no one should ask, "Does this outfit make me look fat?"

What to Expect From the Schizoid Boss

Do not expect to find this boss in a company that depends highly on warm, social interactions with clients and the public. Instead, look for them in engineering firms or technological development companies. Because of their successful understanding of inanimate working parts, SPDs often are promoted to management positions. Like the Dependent Personality Disorder boss, the SPD bullies others not by overt, aggressive actions, but by the lack of action.

CASE STUDY: DANIEL

"I've never just up and quit a job like this before. I know my job and I know how to follow instructions and be a team player. But it's hard to follow instructions if you don't receive any, and it's hard to be part of a team if there isn't one."

Daniel is a 35-year-old architectural draftsman in midsize company that receives subcontract work from many local architectural firms. He transferred from his hometown branch of the company to a larger branch in a much larger city. Daniel has an excellent work performance history and is well liked by his coworkers. Since his arrival at the new workplace, he has had difficulty working with his new boss, Kevin.

"There are 20 of us in the office, all supervised by 'The Flying Dutchman.'" This is their term for Kevin; like the doomed ghost ship, Kevin is rarely seen; when he is, it spells disaster for someone in the office. "He's good at his job," said Daniel, "but I don't think I've heard him say more than a sentence a day. Open-door policy? Forget it. He stays away from us, and we do the same. He never plans office birthday or holiday get-togethers; we do, and he never shows or even apologizes for not going."

"When the Dutchman does appear, there's trouble. It usually is because of some harmless, nitnoid error that makes no difference in the project, but he makes a huge deal out of it. He gives us no directions, and then has a fit if we make the smallest mistake. To keep us all productive, so he says, we're not allowed to leave the premises during our lunch hour in case we get stuck in traffic and are late getting back. God forbid we should lose ten minutes of work time.

"Plus, Kevin has no concept of 'praise in public, criticize in private.' Once he came to Marie's desk and, in front of everyone, griped at her for 15 minutes about using the wrong symbol for a pipe outlet. Finally, Marie was so embarrassed that she started to cry. Kevin either didn't notice or didn't care; he just kept on."

CASE STUDY: DANIEL

"This guy is no leader. If we ask him a question about a project, he just mumbles something to get us out of his office. It's not that he micromanages; he doesn't manage at all. After the Dutchman, I'm senior in the office, so I end up making all the decisions that he should be making. I resent this because he gets paid a lot more than I do for sitting in his office with the door shut, writing memos and e-mails so he doesn't have to show his face among us. Never have I heard him laugh. It's like working for Robocop."

It is believed by mental health researchers that SPDs have a large degree of anger hidden deep inside themselves. This, it is theorized, is why Ted Kaczynski turned from being an odd but harmless recluse into a serial murderer. Kaczynski was deeply angry about the effects of too much technology upon the environment. Like Kaczynski, Daniel's boss, Kevin, bullied others at a distance. A useful example of the Schizoid Personality Disorder and the Antisocial Personality Disorder, both supreme bullies in the workplace, is executed serial murderer John Gacy. A predatory ASPD, he killed 32 young men with his own hands and buried them in the crawlspace under his house. Ted Kaczynski, an SPD, killed three people and attempted to kill 23 more people at a distance, mailing his bombs to individuals that offended his feelings about the environment.

> "Over a 17-year history, Ted Kaczynski, the so-called Unabomber, killed three people and wounded 23 others. Although he probably had other psychological disorders, the Unabomber represents a good example of an individual with the Schizoid Personality Disorder. And although the vast majority of schizoids are not violent, his case history reveals many similarities with other schizoid types."
> **—Cavaiola & Lavender**

It is highly unlikely that a boss like Kevin would resort to homicide in the workplace. Yet, in their way, SPD bosses bully others mercilessly by their aloof withdrawal, lack of leadership, inattention to employees' needs, and by forcing subordinates to keep the office ball rolling. These bosses do not realize that they are bullies, but in its own way, having a SPD like Kevin as a boss is akin to receiving a package in the mail from Ted Kaczynski.

What to Expect From the Schizoid Coworker

Employees can easily pick up that they are working alongside an SPD coworker; they will feel as if they come to work each day in a large mansion with empty rooms. Commonly, the following is a list of expectations when working with an SPD:

- Do not expect to make or feel a personal connection with the coworker; such is unwanted and intolerable for him.

- He will do his utmost to stay invisible in the workplace, engaging with coworkers only if it cannot be avoided. Do not push it; a blank stare will be his reaction to friendly overtures.

- Expect to be bored, wanting only to ignore him.

- He will seem cold and impersonal, speaking only when spoken to.

- Do not expect him to talk about his personal or family life; he almost certainly has neither.

- Coworkers should not talk to him about their personal or family life; he does not care.

- The SPD coworker hates to have his workspace or his isolation intruded upon (consider Kaczynski's hidden shack in an uninhabited area of the mountains). This includes attendance at office functions; he would not be there.

- It is best not to touch an SPD coworker; even a friendly handshake is an intrusion.

- Learn to be comfortable with silence; it is his nature and no reflection on anyone else.

The SPD coworker's form of workplace bullying is unique and difficult to recognize.

CASE STUDY: RAPHAEL

"Vernon and I have shared a cubicle at work for over a year," said Raphael. "In all that time, I don't think he's spoken more than one complete sentence to me. He's cold, unsmiling, and focuses on nothing but work tasks.

"Just to show him how silly he was being, I started writing him funny e-mails; he never responded although he was only four feet away. We often were given projects to complete together. Vernon was so unapproachable, I didn't even talk to him about the project tasks; I just did all of them myself. It was worth it, just to not have to deal with him. He never asked about the tasks, like nothing existed but him. Vernon's not lazy; he's just not capable of working with coworkers. So most of his work gets done by me and others. We just shut up and let it be."

Raphael fell victim to the SPD coworker's workplace bully's best tactic: becoming so aloof and unreachable that other learn to keep the peace by just going along.

The Schizoid Subordinate

SPD subordinates are difficult to manage because of the complaints about them that a boss must work through. The boss must also be able to recognize SPD traits when he or she sees them, especially as a form of workplace bullying. The SPD subordinate excels at working with technology, not with people. If forced into a role where he regularly meets with clients and/or potential clients, this subordinate will not be a good ambassador for the company. He will most likely indirectly bully another employee into unwillingly taking on this task by calling in sick or having a "family emergency." This is also a form of bullying the boss, since he or she will be manipulated into giving the SPD only technical tasks, while overloading other employees with extra work.

The Avoidant

Many employees in a workplace may not know that there is an Avoidant Personality Disorder (APD) in their midst; they are there, but rooting them out of their office hiding places is a daunting task. APDs keep themselves out of any situation that might bring them into the open. Office meetings, parties, presentations, and promotion or retirement ceremonies that cause and APD to be "on public display" are not only terrifying but also strictly avoided at all costs. Believing themselves to be failures, incompetent, and inadequate personally and professionally, all the APD wants to do is disappear into oblivion. In its most pathological form, APDs do not seek employment of any kind where they might have to deal with others. In fact, many APDs do not work outside the home unless they are forced to for economic reasons. It has been speculated among mental health researchers that the state welfare and disability rolls may be heavily populated by APDs who cannot cope with a public workplace; however, this is still under research and is strictly speculation at this time.

Avoidants have an unshakeable belief that if they were more visible in the workplace, others would discover their secret: they are inadequate and incompetent and should be fired at once. This type of rejection is intolerable for the APD; they can only tolerate situations where they are certain that they are liked and viewed in a positive light.

The APD employee and the Schizoid Personality Disorder have some commonalities; the difference between them is based on the facts that the SPD *does not want* interaction with others, while the avoidant *does*, but is ruled by fear of being rejected. The avoidant also feels emotions such as happiness and affection for others, while the SPD does not. Unlike the oblivious SPDs, the APDs are constantly scanning social situations that could result in criticism or abandonment; the SPD cannot be bothered to know or care what others think of him.

The DSM-IV-TR describes the Avoidant Personality Disorder as follows:

- Avoids occupational activities that involve significant interpersonal contact because of fears of criticism, disapproval, or rejection

- Unwilling to get involved with people unless they are certain they will be liked

- Shows restraint in intimate relationships because of the fear of being shamed or ridiculed

- Preoccupation with being criticized or rejected in social situations

- Inhibited in interpersonal situations because of feelings of inadequacy

- View themselves as socially inept, personally unappealing, or inferior to others

- Reluctant to take personal risks or engage in any new activities because they may prove embarrassing

FAVORITE REPLIES OF THE AVOIDANT BOSS

1. I will take your ideas under advisement.

2. I will let you know.

3. Could you write this idea/request as a memo?

4. I will take care of it.

5. Let us get some opinions from others.

6. I will get back to you.

CASE STUDY: SAMANTHA

"I met Jan at work," Samantha told her counselor. "I was new on the job and I liked her right away. We did the same kind of accounting work for the company; we weren't in competition with each other. I saw her as an equal, a mentor, and I hoped, as a potential friend.

"My second week at work, I asked her to have lunch with me. She ducked her head and politely said thanks, but she didn't know me well enough yet. In the next weeks, Jan seemed very upset by the way I did my work — as if she was afraid I was better than her. She started really staying away from me, wherever I was or what I was doing.

"I had this weird reaction; if I did something well and got compliments from our boss, I never told her about it. I was afraid to let her know that I'd gotten good performance reports. Why is that? Other people would be happy for

CASE STUDY: SAMANTHA

me, but Jan just seemed scared. I didn't want her job — I had my own job and it was just like hers. She did a great job, so what was she worrying about?

"Now she never talks to me at all. I keep thinking it's my fault; I must've done something wrong. But what? Why should I apologize for doing my work well? And pardon me for asking Jan to lunch, which she never took me up on."

What to Expect From the Avoidant Boss

Nothing. Employees are on their own with this boss. Regularly a female Caucasian, this boss came into a management position because of her considerable technical skills rather than her leadership or management skills. She does not like meetings and individual feedback sessions with subordinates. Expect that this boss will lead via e-mails and written memos, not verbal communication. She prefers a "hands-off" management approach.

The avoidant boss, like the dependent boss, bullies through indirect, almost absent-minded tactics. When asked to make decisions and set guidelines in the workplace, she will put off doing it and thereby adds to daily tension and frustration in the office. Replies will be noncommittal and indistinct, leaving the concerned subordinate wondering what was accomplished in any face-time with the avoidant boss. Most often, not a thing.

All this makes for some very frustrated and angry subordinates, who resort to the only resolution possible; they make decisions and set policies themselves. Far from being annoyed, the avoidant boss is actually and secretly pleased with this turn of events since it saves them from doing what they hate the most: leading others through hands-on management. The APD boss bullies through inaction, until such inaction can no longer be ignored. It should be noted that the problem with bullying avoidant bosses is not simply that they do not *want* to lead; it is also that they do not know *how* to lead. Recognizing this dynamic, the senior manager often tries to remedy the problem by sending the APD boss to leadership training seminars — none of which seem to make the slightest difference. The reason for this stalemate lies in the very distinct definition of a personality disorder as previously mentioned: a *pervasive pattern of character* that is "hard-wired" into the individual and not subject to reversal.

This old gag describes the APD boss perfectly; she does not really want to change. She prefers to avoid interactions and, by her pervasive pattern of inaction and avoidance, bully subordinates into doing her job. As technically skilled as she may be, this is no assistance for the subordinate whose perpetual cry is "This is not my job!"

Neither is the APD boss likely to be the champion of her subordinates' favorite projects, promotions, or raises. This behavior does not occur maliciously, as in other personality-disordered bosses, but again out of her unease with interactions that are necessary with others to accomplish these personnel management tasks. This, too, could be considered as a form of bullying to make subordinates stop bothering her, but most often is it merely a symptom of the APD boss.

What to Expect From the Avoidant Coworker

CASE STUDY: ROD

"I've worked with Anna for four years," Rod explained, "and I know absolutely nothing about her. Boyfriend, husband, kids, community fun stuff — beats me. She never says one word about herself and her life, and never asks me about mine."

CASE STUDY: ROD

"I got the surprise of my life when the boss congratulated her in a staff meeting for passing the bar exam. None of us even knew she was in law school at night! We're paralegals and know just how hard this is, much less sitting for the bar exam. Funny, but instead of smiling when the boss congratulated her, she seemed embarrassed at the attention. If I passed the bar, I'd rent a billboard and throw a party! Anna just blushed and ducked her head.

"She'd been the firm's senior partner's paralegal for several years, specializing in contract and real estate law. Anna and I had a system that seemed to work for both of us, even though it struck me as odd. When we had a new client, I conducted all the initial interviews with the client and witnesses and drew up very detailed notes on the case. Then Anna took it all over and did the research, wrote the briefs, and made all the court filings. And she was really talented at these tasks, much better than I was. On the other hand, in a client interview she seemed to freeze up and essential matters weren't addressed.

"At least we have a workable solution in the office, but a little conversation would be nice. Sometimes it can get a little intense at work for people who don't know Anna. Last summer a colleague's teenage daughter was killed in a car wreck; everyone attended the funeral and sent flowers to the family except Anna. She did send a card, but the girl's father told me later that at least Anna could have personally expressed her sympathy. It's not that Anna didn't care; she didn't know how to say so. I like Anna, and I understand how she is. But sometimes I feel that she over-relies on me to do work that she should be doing, like interviewing clients and witnesses. She knows that I know she won't or can't do it and that I'll end up eventually doing something that's part of her job. Sometimes I feel that she's taking advantage of me."

Rod and his colleagues are dealing with an APD in their workplace, another subtle bully who knows that her behavior will be tolerated because it is simply easier this way. She is not lazy or technically unskilled; she is unwilling to risk failure or rejection from others. She means no harm, but causes it nonetheless.

The APD coworker bully is manifested in yet another manner: this is the coworker who has decided that one colleague alone can be trusted not to reject or criticize her. Although she can be a loyal friend, this coworker will cling to her target for constant support and assurance. Having no self-confidence, this coworker bullies her target by demanding a large portion of the target's time. At first, the target plays it off, not really minding. Yet as time goes by, the target becomes increasingly weary of the APD coworker's demands for time and emotional support and exactly what the APD fears comes to pass: her incessant neediness makes others turn away and reject her. "You can't have my life! My life is already taken — by me! If you need a therapist, then get one!" is a refrain that the target of the APD could easily understand; what seemed like a friendship with a slightly fragile person eventually evolved into a one-way parasitic interaction. When the target does finally reject this coworker, it merely serves to reinforce what she knew all along; that she is incompetent, disliked, inadequate, and not worthy of recognition. Like the schizoid and dependent bullying coworker, the APD can be just as insidious as the narcissist and the antisocial, who wound on purpose and with pleasure.

CONSTANT QUESTIONS BY THE AVOIDANT FACING A SOCIAL SITUATION	
1. What should I wear?	6. Will I embarrass myself?
2. Does this make me look fat?	7. How can I get out of this?
3. Do I need to lose/gain weight?	8. Should I pretend I'm sick?
4. Am I attractive?	9. What if they don't like me?
5. Will they like me?	10. What if I say the wrong thing?

What to Expect From the Avoidant Subordinate

Depending upon the patience level and the personal and professional energy of the boss of an APD subordinate, the avoidant's excessive need for reassurance and assistance may cause her presence in the workplace to be a short one. Fast-moving, intense workplaces simply do not have the time to continually nurture a subordinate who is clingy, uncertain of herself, and emotionally demanding. These bullies operate on a premise of "I need help; am I doing okay?" not occasionally, but time and time again. They may be hired because of their work skills, but tend not to last long. Smaller-paced companies and bosses are more tolerant of the APD subordinate, but the complaints of other workers tend to surface quickly.

QUESTION: *How many therapists does it take to change a light bulb?*
ANSWER: *Only one, but the bulb has to really want to change.*
— **A Therapist's Proverb**

She is not unpleasant or competitive. She is eager to please, but completely lacking in interpersonal skills. This is a fatal flaw if the company requires her to interact with the public; she creates a very poor impression upon current and future clients. Moving her to another section in the company will not help; it will merely cause additional problems since the APD has such difficulty when she is thrust among strangers.

At company social functions, this subordinate will be the last to arrive and the first to depart, if she arrives at all. Knowing that a function looms in her future, she will call in sick or schedule vacation days to avoid attending a function. Unless she is certain of being liked and accepted, the APD subordinate will avoid any social function. Of course, it is impossible to be certain that one will be liked and accepted because of the vast array of personal characteristics, interests, and "pet peeves." The APD is doomed to experience extreme anxiety because what she hopes for will never come to pass.

The APD subordinate bullies through helplessness, either real or feigned. She is often much more competent than she lets on, but her lack of self-esteem makes her constantly question her abilities. Like all avoidants, she bullies her boss by her excessive need for his or her time and continual reassurance. Because she is pleasant and endearing, her boss will initially provide help, support, and reassurance at first, believing that her clingy helplessness will end once she settles into her job. This does not happen, and the boss finds herself spending too much time mentoring this one person. The APD does not benefit from job performance evaluations; she merely uses the poor evaluation as a means to cement her own ideas of her incompetence. A weary boss may give in to this subtle bullying and forgo performance evaluations altogether — the desired outcome of the APD bullying subordinate. It is not uncommon for an avoidant to quit a job just before she believes (correctly) that she is about to be fired. Thus, employers who interview a competent, skilled individual who has had numerous short-term jobs should be on the watch for signs of avoidance.

Just Plain Mean (JPM)

Not all toxic workplace bullies fall into the category of having a personality disorder. On the contrary, there are many bosses, coworkers, and subordinates who simply enjoy being mean because they can. These bullies unerringly find their vulnerable target, and barrage him or her with sheer venom. They do not meet the full DSM-IV-TR diagnostic criteria for any specific type of personality disorder although they may have traits or features of the Narcissistic or Antisocial Personality Disorders. Clinically, these vicious bullies may fall into the DSM-IV-TR category of Personality Disorder Not Otherwise Specified (NOS), meaning that, for example, they have the sense of narcissistic entitlement, mean-spiritedness of the antisocial, chaotic relationships of the borderline, or another mish-mash of pervasive patterns of personality characteristics.

CASE STUDY: LUKE

"This organization of mine has a few individuals that could be called bullies," said Luke, a senior employee. "If one person fits the bill, it's Dave, not affectionately known as 'Dirty' because that's how he is in every aspect. Dirty is given special treatment because, as a handicapped government employee, it takes an act of Congress to fire his sorry ass."

"The boss gives him any jobs that will take him out of the building so he's not bothering the rest of us. This gives him plenty of time to (expletive) off and do as he pleases. When he's in the shop performing his main duty, he's never asked to assist the section because of his constant negative comments. My coworker Julie is constantly watching her intake of food, exercising religiously, taking a conscientious approach to her diet and fitness, and works hard. Dirty, never short on anything to say especially if it's negative, makes his daily speech of antigovernment comments about our abundance of sick leaves.

"In walks Julie with a McDonald's bag. She opens it, unwraps a breakfast sandwich, and sounds off about how busy she was last night and that she didn't eat dinner, so she was starving. She said she has been assisting in someone else's section and that she was finally looking forward to eating. No sooner than she had taken the first bite when Dirty goes off on her for eating so unhealthy, that she needs to be on a diet, that she will always be fat, and no matter how hard she exercises it won't make any difference. He continues on, even though she is visibly hurt from his barrage. She removes

CASE STUDY: LUKE

the food from her mouth and puts it back into the wrapper. She is crying hard because of his comments, throws her sandwich away and walks out of the office to the women's restroom to get away from him and everyone else.

"Julie told me that she felt ambushed by him and didn't see it coming because she had always thought of Dave as a friend. I wasn't surprised about what he'd done because he often goes off on things unrelated to him and for some reason he feels it necessary to share his unasked-for input. I even liked him for a while until I started watching what he did to people. Then I realized how mean and negative he actually is. This thing with Julie opened my eyes."

Examining Dave's behavior as Luke related it, it is difficult to find more than a few personality disorder traits. Nevertheless, he chose Julie as his vulnerable target of bullying; Julie was struggling with her weight and fitness as many military members do. Dave painted the proverbial bullseye on this vulnerability and made a straight shot right into what hurts her the most. Dave's JPM behavior extended to making negative comments about a military organization that supports and defends his country at great personal sacrifices.

This is not pathological; it is simply rude and offensive. As a JPM individual, Dave has the poor manners to "trash talk" anyone he pleases. It is also interesting to notice that "Dirty" chose Julie, a woman, for his bullying target. This is often true of male JPM individuals; they bully women instead of "manning up" to a male. If they do target a male for their bullying, it is always a male who, for some reason, will not defend himself from being bullied. The JPM bully who chooses a male as a target is likely to find that, when the boss looks away, justice was served. Problem solved. The JPM individual will "be cool" for a while, and then choose another, more vulnerable, target.

CASE STUDY: TED

"My mother died suddenly two years ago," said Ted. "Prior to her death, she worked as a customer service reception for a nationally known hotel chain. She was in her 60s, older than her two supervisors. Mom had a host of issues that prevented her from being a 'poster employee' for any job. Mom liked to talk on a personal level to corporate customers instead of following the standard script that was provided for her; this was her warm personality coming through. So there was always a conflict between her and her supervisor."

"Also, Mom was a bit more educated than the 'kids' who supervised her. Maybe they considered her to be a threat to them. Mom's only goal was to use her skills to pay her debts and provide for the necessities of life. She found that her supervisor looked over her shoulder throughout the course of her time at work. Mom exhausted herself to conform to her supervisor's expectations, only to have another supervisor inform her that she was doing her job incorrectly.

"They nitpicked her for being unprofessional, even though she only talked with customers on the phone. Mom was overweight, walked slowly with a cane, and was not always made up appropriately. What did that matter, since she had no direct contact with customers? These supervisors actually threatened my mom, saying that all she had to do is say something they didn't like, and she would be gone.

"Mom worked overtime, and was not paid for this; they told her that if she didn't work overtime, she needn't report for her regular duty schedule. I visited Mom from time to time at work, just to let these supervisors know that someone cared about her and that I 'had her back' anytime she wanted to confront them about their abusive treatment of her. She was only paid minimum wage and they kept her hours under part-time, so she wasn't eligible for full-time benefits. My mom endured it.

"Then the time came where she had to have surgery and was off for only a week for her recuperation. On the first day back to work — way ahead of

CASE STUDY: TED

her doctor's recommendations — she was fired within an hour of her arrival for her shift.

"This type of behavior always shows its ugly head. Those who have the power to alter or change a subordinate's life abuse their power. Mom has since passed away, and I miss her; she was important in my life. I loved her, and I know she loved me."

The JPM target is unerringly aimed in bright red in the direction of the JPM's vulnerabilities. Ted's story is indicative of mixed personality traits that all too often result in malicious workplace bulling. Ted's vignette is a pointy reflection of an eldest son's perceived lack of courage, but also as a reflection of how employees who are different from their coworkers are bullied simply because they are different. Difference, in the workplace, is seldom tolerated. The mean-spirited but not pathologic actions of these workplace bullies often result in either individual bullying or mob bullying, which will be discussed in detail later in this book.

"All cruelty springs from weakness."
— Seneca (4 BC)

In conclusion to this chapter on the characteristics of workplace bullies, it is important to keep in mind that many features of a personality disorder are rampant among bullying bosses, coworkers, and subordinates. Nature versus nurture: No one yet knows the answers to these questions raised by therapists, court intake officers, and juvenile court judges. We may constantly ask these questions and still find no substantiated answers. For now, bosses, coworkers, and subordinates must simply understand what they are dealing with and then do the best that they can under the circumstances.

"Evil is that force, residing either inside or outside human beings, that seeks to kill life or loveliness. Those with evil personalities use power to destroy the spiritual growth of others for the purpose of defending and preserving the integrity of their own sick selves."

— Dr. M. Scott Peck
People of the Lie

Chapter 3

Profiles of Targets of Workplace Bullies

To fully understand a bully, we must also understand the bully's targets. A target may not realize that he or she is actually being bullied by a boss, coworker, or subordinate. Targeted employees do understand that something is horribly wrong in their workplace, but tend to ascribe their own misery to their own incompetence and that they are the cause of their misery, not the bullying boss, coworker, or subordinate. This tendency to absorb the bully's wrongdoing and then blame themselves for being bullied is a primary characteristic of targets. If an individual is constantly barraged with verbal and written reprimands about his or her job performance, a vulnerable target will eventually come to accept this as truth instead of recognizing these bullying actions for what they are.

Namie and Namie (2000) refer to being the target of bullying as "an undeserved burden." Bullies do not target everyone in the workplace, only those who are vulnerable for a variety of reasons such as age, gender, degree of skill, personality characteristics, the degree of the bully's own feelings of inadequacy, the positions in the workplace of the target and the bully, and the bully's ability to harm the target without being punished. Targets are "Everyman" according to the Namies' research:

- 21 percent of targets have a graduate or professional degree

- 63 percent of targets have some college or an undergraduate degree

- Targets tend to be independent, bright, and skilled individuals

- 50 percent of employers that tolerate bullying are in private sector businesses; 33 percent are governmental agencies, and 19 percent are nonprofit organizations

The Namies also cite the top four reasons for being bullied:

- The target refuses to be subservient or overcontrolled

- The bully envies the target's superior competence

- The bully envies the target's social skills, being liked, and positive attitude

- The target is an ethical, whistleblower-type employee

Some bullies can act so subtly that the target is unsure if he or she is actually being bullied, or if the bully's behavior is merely a personality trait that is unleashed on everyone, not just the target. Answering some simple questions about the workplace environment and the bully's actions will help a targeted employee make this determination.

1) Does your coworker or supervisor frequently seem irritated or angry with you several times a week?

2) Do you feel confused because your very best work meets with constant criticism?

3) Are you distressed about your work environment?

4) Do you feel that your attempts at communication are constantly ignored, misunderstood, or degraded?

5) Do you blame yourself for your boss's or coworker's criticism?

6) Have you begun to doubt your competence and skill at work?

7) Does your boss leave you out of plans and information that is essential for you to correctly do your job, and then criticize you for not doing the job correctly?

8) Does your boss or coworker angrily deny the problem between you if you attempt to discuss it?

9) Have you noticed an increase in stress-related symptoms like insomnia, anorexia, depression, anxiety, overeating, increased smoking, or alcohol use and irritability?

10) Do you feel singled out at work for harsh criticism, often in public?

Susan Futterman (2004) takes a slightly different approach for an individual to determine if he has become the target of a bully, noting that interactions between bullies and the targets are merely a "series of disasters" where the target is liberally coated with abuse but has no opportunity or workplace forum for rebuttal or mediation. Futterman's list focuses only upon bullying bosses.

1) Your manager consistently imposes arbitrary verbal and written warnings and/or disciplinary procedures that are unjustified, without reason, and directed solely to you.

2) Your positive contributions to the workplace are not acknowledged.

3) Your attempts at initiative and independent thinking are vigorously discouraged.

4) Minor flaws and imperfections in your work performance are magnified out of proportion, and keep getting "thrown up to you." The past is also the present.

5) Your manager bypasses you in giving instructions to your subordinates.

6) You are good at your job, and thereby a threat to your manager.

7) You are required more and more often to justify your decisions and actions by writing copious memos to the manager; the timeliness of your work suffers because of this and then you are chastised for not meeting deadlines (The "Gotcha!" bullying tactic).

8) You feel that your autonomy in the workplace is declining because your manager constantly micromanages you.

9) You are liked and respected by your colleagues and subordinates.

10) You are older than your manager, with more job experience.

11) You are considerably younger than your manager and assumed to be unskilled and incompetent because of your youth.

12) You are capable of self-motivation and intuition, needing little management.

13) You do not participate in office politics.

CASE STUDY: SHELLY

Shelly worked for a large governmental agency. She worked for the agency for 15 years as a mid-level manager with very good performance reports. Shelly was recently transferred to another branch office. Her initial evaluation of her boss and her coworkers and subordinates was positive; she looked forward to her new workplace. "All seemed well at first. I felt welcome by everyone." But in only a month, the problems began.

"My boss seemed like someone I could trust and confide in. I told her that sometimes I had problems with self-esteem when it came to managing my subordinates. This was because two years ago I had an episode of major depression, for which I still took medication. I shared with her that my son died of leukemia, and this is what triggered my depression. Although she expressed sympathy and support, something changed that day. She started to treat me like I needed constant micromanagement. Any small mistake she turned into a huge problem with my overall performance. Everyone but me was allowed to make a mistake now and then. She told me that because of my depression, I was not a self-starter and that's why she had to use all her time managing me.

"I don't like office gossip; I just do my job and mind my business. My boss said I was isolated and withdrawn. She said she couldn't trust me to follow through with work projects, so she started to bypass me and tell my subordinates what to do. She actually told them that I had many 'personal problems' and that we should all try to help. They liked me, and told me about this. When I confronted my boss about doing this, she said, 'Why are you blaming me for your problems?' I replied, 'I don't have any problems except you.' She gave me a written reprimand for being rude and insubordinate, and I guess I was because I lost my temper."

CASE STUDY: SHELLY

"At our next staff meeting, she gave this long, rambling speech about how she wouldn't tolerate disrespect from anyone no matter what their position. Everyone knew she was talking about me. After that, a new employee whom I supervised abruptly quit. His letter of resignation stated that he found our workplace to be unpleasant and distressing. My boss told me that I had caused an employee with great potential to quit. That did it!

"Hardly a day went by that she wasn't criticizing or reprimanding me for something. Sometimes, she said things loudly enough to be overheard by others. She was very nice to other employees, especially my subordinates; I seemed to be her special whipping child. She kept telling me that my depression was causing all my so-called problems, and that I'd 'better get my head together.' I started to wonder if she was right about my depression causing my incompetence, so I told my psychiatrist about all this. He had me complete a couple of questionnaires about my symptoms and talked with me for a long time. Finally, he said that he saw no increase in my depression, but that I was under way too much stress. Just to be safe, he increased my antidepressant dose.

"I don't know how my boss found out about this — someone in our benefits office must have told her but nobody ever admitted it. My boss had an 'I told you so' attitude about this increased dose; she told me to be grateful that she was right all along. The harassment and abuse continued. When I had the flu, she told my subordinates that I wasn't really ill, I just couldn't handle my responsibilities so I faked being sick to stay home. When my computer broke down, she said, 'How convenient' and reprimanded me for failing to meet a deadline. My psychiatrist advised me to see an attorney about all this, and I did. My attorney called the company's chief and told him that if this harassment didn't stop, we would be taking legal action.

"Well, it did stop. My boss called me into her office and told me that she was just going to forget that I worked there since I would 'rat her out' anytime she said or did something that I didn't like. So I became invisible, which was almost as bad as being harassed. I've got eight months until I can retire early with full benefits, and I'm leaving. Until then, I'll just stay invisible."

"Bullies start all conflict and trouble; targets react."

Since 81 percent of workplace bullies are bosses, these individuals are accomplished office politicians. While they may appear to be totally performance oriented, their real primary goal is to control others, especially a targeted employee. Sometimes, an employee does not see that he is being controlled and manipulated. For example, when Shelly's boss began to bypass her, she told Shelly's subordinates that they could help Shelly by coming directly to the boss. In reality, there was no altruistic motive for Shelly's boss to do this; the bullying boss controlled and manipulated Shelly's subordinates in trying to convince them that an unacceptable workplace practice was done only to "help" Shelly.

Namie & Namie cite ten bullying tactics that, if observed, let the target be certain that he or she is being bullied by a boss:

- Blaming the target for "errors" that may not even exist

- Unreasonable job demands, e.g., a heavy workload or additional work hours

- Criticism of the target's abilities

- Inconsistent compliance with company rules and policies

- Threats of job loss

- Insults and put-downs, sometimes publically

- Discounting or denying a target's accomplishments

- Exclusion of the target from information

- Yelling, swearing, name-calling, and/or body language of disrespect or aggression

- Stealing credit for the target's work

In many ways, a bully is like a lioness stalking her prey. Like the lioness, the bully scans groups searching for the weakest target. It is nature's way that animals that are aged, sick, young, or otherwise vulnerable are culled by predatory hunters. To humans, this may seem very harsh and horrible, yet it is actually merciful and necessary. But people, in general, are not the predators we once were in prehistory. We have become "civilized." We buy our meat in a supermarket, extremely rarely wondering how animals are slaughtered for our dinner tables. Nonetheless, there remain human predators in our midst like murderers, rapists, and child molesters, so it would be foolish indeed for humans to self-righteously say that we are no longer predators. In the workplace, bullies scan the group, especially new employees. What they seek is a target that would not put up much of a fight, or none at all. The bully is not interested in targeting someone who will instinctively and unerringly "bow up" with the bully. Since, to a bully, the workplace becomes a gladiatorial arena where the bully always wins, he or she backs off if a potential target resists. Bullies are basically cowardly and lazy; they do not want to put in the time, effort, and possible defeat when trying to target someone who shows unexpected and strong resistance. "Oh yeah?" the nontarget conveys. "Try it, just bring it on and we'll see who comes out of the arena alive." Wanting only an easy victory, the bullies scuttle off in a hurry to find a more meek and vulnerable target. The lioness, kicked too many times by a battling zebra, backs down to save her energy for an easier mark.

"All predatory species select and attack the weakest prey. Barely human, bullies only symbolically eat their prey. They are gratified by the fear they instill in targets."
— Namie & Namie

The workplace bully has a special set of criteria for selecting a target. Always on the hunt, the bully watches and listens carefully to signals around him or her. Signs of vulnerability can be found in the potential target who is not very self-confident, who makes self-effacing statements that indicate insecurity and overreliance on others, has a meek way of speaking, shows tolerance to being interrupted, and uses words that clearly convey their vulnerability such as, "I'm not very good at this." The bully also scans for vulnerability through actions, like the way the potential target walks, carries herself, stands, uses his hands, and has personal space boundaries. A viable potential target acts meek and unresisting: think of Stephen King's vulnerable character, Carrie White. Sometimes, the bully miscalculates or misjudges the prey's true vulnerability, much as Carrie's bullies misjudged her in King's masterful revenge-oriented style. Nevertheless, an accomplished, serial bully rarely makes this mistake. They also check out the potential target's personal space boundaries; they stand too close, hover, and touch to see what the reaction is. Cowering or tolerating the bully's invasion of their space instantly lets the bully know that this is a person who does not stand a chance in the workplace arena.

In writing on the legal aspect of bullying behavior, attorney Robert Mueller describes workplace bullying as a life style rather than simply an obnoxious and often illegal behavioral pattern. Bullies like and cultivate this life style, as incredible as this sounds to nonbullies. Rather than viewing bullies as predators who carefully analyze potential targets, Mueller believes that targets are chosen at random; if it is not Person A, it would just be Person B. In addition to describing bullying as a life style, Mueller describes it also as a lifelong dedication since bullies, like serial killers, do not stop; they are stopped. Internally, they do not change their thoughts and emotions about the inferiority of others; they merely change their behavior because they got caught.

Mueller describes isolation of the target as the bully's central problem. People, in general, resist isolation except for those suffering from Schizoid Personality Disorder which was presented earlier. To remove support from targets and to demoralize them, bullies must separate them from their coworkers or supervisors. As John Donne indicated in his famous meditation, people tend to band together in many ways like clubs, sports leagues, community organizations, and churches. Bonding with others provides us with feelings of support, safety, and encouragement. Again, Mueller sees this type of banding together as random; people want to be with others who are like them and have similar interests and beliefs, so they naturally congregate just as herds of deer and zebras do. Bonding is natural; isolation is not, among healthy individuals. The bullying boss works against the tide of bonding and cleverly succeeds by "dividing and conquering."

Namie and Namie pose the question — not rhetorical or hypothetical — of whether or not a target knows and understands that he or she is the target of a workplace bully. They answer with a resounding yes. Self-denial allows targets to deny what, in hindsight, is glaringly obvious. Denial is a powerful defense mechanism where we can bury unpleasant thoughts, emotions, problems, or events. Scarlett O'Hara, the unconquerable heroine of *Gone With the Wind*, had a unique way of dealing with the problems of war, starvation, family conflicts, and the loss of Melanie and Rhett Butler: "I can't think about that now. I'll go crazy if I do. I'll think about that tomorrow." Sometimes, this is a good way of not dwelling on the anxieties of the future, the "what ifs..." of our lives. Denial effectively blocks many painful realities of the past, present, and future. For example, consider the controversy over so-called repressed memories of childhood sexual abuse. Whether this type of denial truly exists is a matter of debate for mental health professionals. For the purposes of this book, it is noted as a self-coping mechanism to avoid continual distress about the past. The power of the mind protects us from being overwhelmed by troubling life experiences like abuse, combat, being a violent crime victim, and natural disasters.

With targets of bullying, shame plays a large part in denial. If a target acknowledges and admits that he or she is being bullied in the workplace, the target may see this as shameful and weak. Worse, others in the workplace will see the target as meek and passive. Thus, the target makes many excuses for the bully's behavior such as "Oh, that's just how she is. It doesn't bother me," or "I know what he's doing and I can handle it, " or "I don't have a problem with the way she treats me; if it doesn't bother me, it shouldn't bother anyone else," or "He's not a bully, he's just really intense about his work," or "She's just trying to help me." The denial excuses are endless, but they all amount to relieving the target from feelings of shame and guilt. By accepting and minimizing the bully's behavior, the target saves herself from embarrassment in the workplace. The target may also believe that aggressively confronting the bully will result in the loss of his job. "I'm lucky to have a job at all," is a target in denial's self-depreciating inner mind. For the target to ask himself, "Am I being bullied?" opens the proverbial can of worms that the target, for a variety of reasons, does not want to address. Putting a name to the bully's treatment of the target may not be tolerated. Like the shame and guilt of a rape or incest survivor, a target's prolonged denial only serves to intensify his or her negative self-concept. It does not work in the long term; it only worsens the situation because it allows the bully to continue his or her actions unabated and allows the target to be victimized. For the bullying to stop, the target's denial must be eliminated through acknowledgement and direct confrontation. This concept is frightening for all concerned; the bully faces serious consequences from his own superiors and/or a court of law, and the target must acknowledge the truth of what happened to him or her.

> *"No man is an island, entire of itself; every man is a piece of the continent, a part of the main....any man's death diminishes me, because I am involved in mankind; and therefore never send to know for whom the bell tolls — it tolls for thee."*
> **— John Donne**
> *Meditation XVII*

According to Susan Futterman, friends and family members may notice that something is badly amiss before the target does. While a target is still in denial, others may notice many symptoms or warning signs:

- Depression

- Frequent crying

- Anxiety about going to work

- Mood irritability

- Nervousness

- Shortened attention span

- Stress-related health problems

- Changes in sleeping and eating patterns

- Compulsive seeking of reassurance

- Forgetfulness

- Lethargy

- Clumsiness

- Social withdrawal

- Excessive focus on work

- Fearful behavior (leaving the house, social interactions)

Futterman also notes that the best way to determine if a friend or family member is being bullied is simply to ask him or her in a supportive, nonjudgmental manner. "Can I help?" is a question that may finally loosen the target's denial and the truth will finally come forward.

- Encourage the target to talk about what is happening at work and how he or she feels about it.

- Assist the target in finding patterns of the workplace bullying.

- Encourage the target to start documenting his or her experiences.

- Suggest that the target seek support from professionals such as a physician, a therapist, or an attorney.

- Make it clear to the target that he or she has the support of family and friends.

- Gently remind that target that he or she is a worthy, responsible person; the bullying is only the fault of the bully.

Finally, targets of workplace bullies may have difficulty understanding that the bullying is not about them, except for their vulnerability. All bullying has its roots in the bully's intense, insatiable need to control others. A workplace bully is extremely likely to be a bully at home with a spouse and/or children; family members become targets simply by "being there."

Chapter 4

The Price of
Workplace Bullying

"You can kill a person only once, but when you humiliate him, you kill him many times over."

Business organizations exist to make profits. They are not intended to provide a therapeutic environment for employees; those who need mental health assistance must do so of their own accord. For example, the workplace is an improper place for an employee to continually air his marital woes to other employees and impeding the work tasks of the company. But when an employee is targeted for bullying, not only does the target suffer; the business also suffers. Upper-level managers who dismiss bullying as annoying but harmless do not realize that in doing so, they cause financial harm to the organization. According to Namie & Namie, job stress is estimated to cost American businesses $200-$300 billion each year; this is more than the net profits of the Fortune 500 companies.

- The target suffers more stress-related illness and takes more sick days. Seventy-five to ninety percent of visits to primary care physicians are for stress-related physical conditions. The National Safety Council estimates that one million employees are absent from work on any given day due to stress-related illnesses.

- Demoralization of the target and those employees

who silently witness the bullying results in decreased productivity by all.

- Targets and other employees who quit their job due to bullying must be replaced; training new employees is expensive for the company. These employees often hold the "keys of the kingdom" as far as how things are accomplished within the company. When they leave, this knowledge base leaves with them.

- Health insurance rates rise due to stress-related illness in the company.

- Workers' compensation payments increase. In 2002, California employers paid out almost $1 billion for medical and legal fees.

- Increasingly, civil lawsuits filed by targets must be litigated, costing the company legal fees, court costs, and, if the company loses the suit, the target must be paid actual damages and even punitive damages.

- Attorney Robert Mueller makes the point that the ultimate goal of a workplace bully is the professional demise of the target; nothing less than total destruction will do. Since bullies tend to be midlevel managers, the upper-level managers have little actual contact with the bully and by and large do not even know the target at all. Since the bully is exceedingly clever at disparaging the target, who has no opportunity to defend himself, upper-level managers very seldom make the effort to investigate the validity of the bullying allegations against the target. With a laissez-faire attitude, upper-level managers tend to have the bully "take care of it" so they can move on to the next board meeting.

This approach is not only dangerous and unfair in the extreme, it is also extremely foolish because the upper-level managers remain ignorant of the financial damage that bullying causes, or has the potential to cause, within the profit margin of the organization.

Mueller refers to the employees who perform the major tasks of the company as "Workplace Warriors." These are the individuals who get the job done despite the machinations and distractions caused by the bully in their midst. Seeing that no support has, or will, come from upper-level managers, the Workplace Warriors often band together to support each other, especially the target of a bullying boss. This is a tough task that is often not worth the effort; there are other jobs out there. The Workplace Warriors pay such a high price just to come to work every day, finding a new job is much preferable than standing up and "going the distance" with a bullying boss. Since the company has shown them no loyalty or even concern, they owe none to the company. Let the employee turnover rate eat into the company's profits; this is workplace justice. While "zero tolerance" for bullying within a company is easy to establish and maintain, many CEOs and other upper-level managers do not seem to "get it." Not only do they fail to understand the psychodynamics and behavior of bullying, they fail to see workplace bullying as a financial liability.

Workplace bullies are selfish, vainglorious individuals who either do not know or do not care that they are harming the financial viability of the company. They are loyal only to themselves and their mean-spirited torment of their target. They have an uncanny ability to present themselves as loyal employees concerned only for the welfare of the company while presenting the target as "trouble." Indifference by upper-level managers causes them to unwittingly be pulled onto the bully's side. When the target — stressed beyond tolerance — suffers a physical or emotional breakdown, the bully shrugs and says, "Told you so." In this vicious cycle, the target is victimized once again by upper managers who believe the bully implicitly.

All too frequently, workplace bullying takes a tragic, but sometimes predictable, turn toward workplace violence. This topic will be fully explored later in the book; for now, let it suffice to say that some individuals have an inner fragility that stems from past life events or mental health problems that are violently reactivated by becoming the target of unending bullying. Bullies sense their vulnerability as targets, but cannot know of their inner struggles. Murderous workplace rampages do not occur out of nowhere; they have a distinct cause and cast of characters. Let the company's upper managers beware, then, of this tragic price of workplace bullying. Wrongful death lawsuits by the families of slain employees, including the target, are expensive enough to bring financial ruin to the company.

The target of a workplace bully certainly has no duty to inform the upper-level managers of a company about the financial costs of bullying; targets have their own problems to deal with. For them, every day is a trial by fire and a violation of the soul.

> "It is tremendously traumatic, what has happened to me. It is my whole life, my whole career that these guys were able to throw out. But it is happening every day, everywhere, to a lot of people."
> **Victim's statement contained in**
> **Davenport, Schwartz, and Elliott**

Futterman (2004), Namie & Namie (2000) and Davenport, Schwartz & Elliott (1999) cite extensive lists of physical and emotional damage caused to the target as the effects of bullying. These damages are combined and paraphrased here:

- Profound feelings of confusion, fear, isolation, paranoia, embarrassment, shame, rage, guilt, depression, anxiety, lack of confidence, poor self-esteem, grief, shock, rejection, and worthlessness

- Posttraumatic Stress Disorder (PTSD) and Prolonged Duress Stress Disorder (PDSD)

- Hypervigilance to perceived emotional threats

- Impairment in focus and concentration

- Social withdrawal and isolation

- Suicide attempts and completed suicide

- Substance abuse and other self-destructive habits

- Domestic violence

- Spontaneous crying

- Impairment in cognitive (thinking) abilities to reason and cope with the problem

- Physical symptoms of stress, e.g., heart palpitations, panic attacks, high blood pressure, tension and migraine headaches, chronic fatigue, anorexia, insomnia, nightmares, gastrointestinal problems, muscle tension, dizziness, restlessness, shortness of breath, reduce immune system, peptic ulcers, and malnutrition

This is by no means an all-inclusive list of physical, emotional, and behavior reactions to the extreme stress of workplace bullying. To put the matter into perception, the Workplace Bullying and Trauma Institute (WBTI), founded in 1998 by Namie and

Namie, break down some startling statistics regarding the top 12 consequences for bullied targets:

- Severe anxiety (94 percent)

- Sleep disturbance (84 percent)

- Loss of concentration (82 percent)

- Feeling edgy, easily started, PTSD (80 percent)

- Obsession about the bully's motives and tactics (76 percent)

- Stress headaches (64 percent)

- Avoidance of feelings or places (49 percent)

- Shame or embarrassment that changed lifestyle routines (49 percent)

- Heart palpitations (48 percent)

- Recurrent, intrusive thoughts and memories (46 percent)

- Body aches in muscles and/or joints (43 percent)

- Clinical depression (41 percent)

Some readers of this book and others like it may experience an "Aha!" moment of great intensity. "This is exactly how I felt!" The value of this type of epiphany comes in realizing that bullying is a pervasive problem in our workplaces; 23 million Americans tell virtually the same story and feel similar impacts of being targeted by bullying. Being convinced by the bully that they are the problem, targets misunderstand why they experience the physical manifestations of severe, prolonged stress and the emotional fallout from the psychological violence of bullying.

CASE STUDY: SHARON

"I thought I was losing my mind," Sharon told her therapist. "I couldn't eat or sleep. I lost 40 pounds. I had headaches that brought me to tears. I was diagnosed with irritable bowel syndrome. At night I would lie in bed for hours replaying scenes between me and my boss and thinking about what I should have said or done. If I wasn't crying, I was angry all the time and it affected my marriage. My husband kept asking me why I was punishing him for what other people did to me. It got so bad, we almost divorced."

"I was constantly on the watch for the next attack. I don't know how, or even why, I hauled myself into that office every day. Why didn't I stop it? I just let him abuse me and was too gutless to do anything about it. I thought about suicide a lot. I fantasized about leaving a suicide note that blamed my boss for my death to make him feel bad. But I really don't think he would have felt bad at all; he would have just told everyone that this was proof I was crazy. I smoked more, drank more, and kept to myself. When my sister told me that she didn't recognize me anymore, who I had become, that woke me up that something was really wrong. Maybe it wasn't all about me. Maybe it was time to ask for help before I really did have a meltdown. I somehow knew it would be soon."

"Bullying is hazardous to your health!
It causes physical and psychological injury!
Targets are NOT mentally ill!"
— Namie & Namie

The consequences to the target of severe, prolonged bullying have serious psychological impacts that must be addressed. In particular, various researchers and authors believe that the target may experience Posttraumatic Stress Disorder (PTSD),

Acute Stress Disorder (ASD), and Generalized Anxiety Disorder. These mental health disorders are contained in the previously mentioned DSM-IV-TR. Another condition called Prolonged Duress Stress Disorder (PDSD) is not contained in the DSM-IV-TR and is not formally recognized as a mental illness by the American Psychiatric Association. Yet it should be noted that this "condition" is receiving much focus as a result of workplace bullying.

Posttraumatic Stress Disorder is characterized by:

- The individual has experienced, witnessed, or was confronted with a traumatic event that involved actual or threatened death or serious injury, including the physical integrity of self or others.

- The individual's response to the event involved intense fear, helplessness, or horror.

- The traumatic event is persistently reexperienced by (1) recurrent, intrusive, and distressing recollections of the event, including images, thoughts or perceptions; (2) recurrent, distressing dreams of the event; (3) acting or feeling as if the traumatic event were recurring in the present via reliving the experience, illusions, hallucinations, and flashback episodes; (4) intense psychological distress at exposure to internal or external cues that symbolize or resemble the traumatic event; and (5) physical reactions on exposure to internal or external cues that symbolize or resemble the traumatic event.

- Persistent avoidance of stimuli associated with the trauma and emotional numbing as indicated by (1) efforts to avoid thoughts, feelings, or conversations associated with the trauma; (2) efforts to avoid activities, places, or people that arouse recollections of the trauma; (3) inability to recall an important aspect of the trauma; (4) markedly diminished interest or participation in significant activities; (5) feelings of detachment or estrangement from others; (6) restricted range of moods; and (7) a sense of a foreshortened future.

- Persistent symptoms of increased arousal as indicated by (1) difficulty falling or staying asleep, (2) irritability or outbursts of anger, (3) difficulty concentrating, (4) hyper-vigilance, and (5) an exaggerated startle response.

This definition of PTSD is difficult to digest for a non-mental health clinician. In broad, PTSD occurs most often among combat survivors, prisoners of war, severely abused children, and people exposed to horrific natural disasters. In light of the outbreak of school shootings, these events would also be included in the type of traumatic event that can induce PTSD symptoms. It is an extreme anxiety disorder meant for those who have survived extreme trauma conditions. The application of PTSD as a response to workplace bullying is controversial. Namie and Namie, Futterman, and Davenport, Schwartz, and Elliot do cite PTSD as one impact of workplace bullying. While Davenport et al. cite only scanty tie-ins of bullying to PTSD, Futterman and Namie and Namie give many more details about why this mental health disorder diagnosis applies to targets of severe, prolonged bullying.

Futterman cites a report by the International Labor Organization indicating that research supports the diagnosis of PTSD as it relates to targets of workplace bullying, and these targets respond similarly to victims involved in traumatic disasters. Futterman does acknowledge that no exact, reliable relationship has been established between the diagnosis of PTSD and targets of workplace bullying.

Namie and Namie, both Ph.D.s (clinical and social psychologists) are much more emphatic in their stance that bullying-induced Acute Stress Disorder (presented below) makes the risk of the development of PTSD more likely. Specifically, this risk is highest when the stress is sudden, severe, prolonged, repetitive, and humiliates the victim or destroys the victim's community and support system. Bullying, they assert, does all these things. It creates hyper-vigilance, thought obsessions and emotional flatness — all symptoms of PTSD. It is curious to note that Namie and Namie are emphatic that targets of bullying are not mentally ill, yet they would attach to targets the clinically significant diagnosis of PTSD, a serious mental disorder. Considering their work in context, it becomes clearer that their intention is to convey that targets of bullying are not bullied because they are mentally ill, but that they become that condition as a result of being bullied. When employees begin new jobs, they are pleasantly excited by the prospect of fresh possibilities, meeting new colleagues, and enjoying their productive time in the new workplace. The last thing they expect is that these merry hopes and anticipations will be shattered by the cruel reality of becoming targets of workplace bullying.

Recognizing that PTSD is an emotional injury that results from an overwhelming psychological assault on the mind, it should be noted that the type of trauma referred to in the PTSD diagnostic criteria contained in the DSM-IV-TR is an event beyond the normal range or ordinary human experience. Seventy-eight percent of Americans describe their jobs as stressful. In light of this statistic, it is difficult to conclude that workplace bullying, as traumatizing as it is, is beyond the normal range of our experiences. Further, if 23 million Americans experience workplace bullying, it becomes still more difficult to compare this insidious practice with the violence of war, terrorism, mass murder, severe abuse, or devastation through a natural disaster. In short, a diagnosis of PTSD is reserved among clinical mental health practitioner for rare, unique events. It was never meant to become the "disease of the week." It is this author's stance that the impact of the trauma inflicted upon the target of workplace bullying very rarely, if ever, qualifies for the clinical label of the mental disorder of PTSD.

According to the DSM-IV-TR, Acute Stress Disorder is almost identical to PTSD, except that ASD is milder in its symptomology and occurs closer in time to the traumatic event. PTSD can have a late onset — months or even years after the trauma. ASD usually shows itself within days or up to four weeks after the traumatic event. ASD is a new addition to the fourth edition of the DSM, not contained in previous editions. It replaced the category of Brief Reactive Psychosis, defined as a stress-induced psychotic state that is time-limited and not the result of a long-standing psychotic disorder.

The DSM-IV-TR defines General Anxiety Disorder (GAD) as follows:

- Excessive anxiety and worry about a number of events or activities such as work or school performance

- The individual finds it difficult to control the worry

- The anxiety and worry are associated with at least three of the following symptoms: (1) restlessness, feeling keyed-up or on edge; (2) being easily fatigued; (3) difficulty concentrating or their minds going blank; (4) mood irritability; (5) muscle tension; and (6) sleep disturbance

- The focus of the anxiety and worry is not related to another mental health disorder

- The anxiety, worry or physical symptoms cause significant distress or impairment in social, occupational, or other important areas of functioning

- The disturbance is not caused by the physiological effects of a substance or medical condition

CASE STUDY: SAMUEL

Samuel is a 44-year-old sales manager for a large electronics store. He sought treatment for anxiety due to intense job stress. "I can't stop fretting. I can't eat or sleep. I'm always worrying about every little thing, like whether my daughter might be kidnapped or molested or my wife will run away with another man. Maybe I have cancer and don't know it. What if we all die in our sleep from carbon dioxide poisoning?"

"Last week our puppy developed an abscess on her face that swelled to the size of a baseball. I was sure she would die. When I took her to the vet, he said he needed to drain the infection and she would be just fine on antibiotics. I didn't believe him. I thought for sure that she had the flesh-eating bacteria and would die, and we would all catch it from her and die too. How goofy is all that?

"I don't understand why I can't quit worrying. It all started about eight months ago. I don't have a good relationship with the store manager, my boss. He nags me and criticizes me every single day. I can't do anything right. He tells me, in front of the clerks, that I won't last long at this job. Everybody makes mistakes now and then, and I'm not saying that I'm perfect. But he makes a huge deal out of the smallest thing I do wrong. He told me that he's keeping a file on me. What does that mean? The more he harasses me, the more I mess up. I think that's what he wants. I feel tired all the

CASE STUDY: SAMUEL

time, but I can't sleep because I just lie there worrying. So it's hard to keep my mind on the job. I know this sounds strange, but I worry about how much I'm worrying. I know it isn't normal."

Although Samuel was diagnosed with Generalized Anxiety Disorder and received antianxiety medication, this was merely a way of easing his severe symptoms. The root of Samuel's difficulty was that he was the target of workplace bullying. More than any other anxiety disorder, GAD is very often linked to job stress that results from being bullied. Anxiety is also linked to physical symptoms of stress like headaches, muscle tension, high blood pressure, heart palpitations, and gastric distress. In addition, anxiety is intrapersonally contagious; worrying about one situation is easily transferred to worrying about other situations however unreal the worry may seem. Thus, a target of workplace bullying who suffers the impact of intense anxiety about his or her work performance and job security may very well begin to worry about any number of other matters, however remote and unlikely the worry may be. If the primary source of worry is extinguished − if the bullying stops − other worries are also very likely to cease. GAD is a significant but treatable condition through medication and therapy. Yet no pharmaceutical or the most skilled therapist can remove the root cause of the patient's distress − the bully.

Posttraumatic Stress Disorder originated in 1980 among the medical and psychiatric community to describe the clinical profile of a severely traumatized person, primarily Vietnam veterans, emergency "first responders" like firefighters who witness the death of a child, or police officers whose partner was killed in the line of duty. In 1994, two British psychologists and researchers, Michael Scott and Stephen Strandling, noted that although some individuals who are the targets of workplace bullying exhibit symptoms of PTSD, their trauma does not result from a single event, but from prolonged victimization by the bully. Targets, they determined, suffer from the impact of being bullied over long periods of time, with no single event standing out as the cause of their distress. Scott and Strandling referred to this distress as Prolonged Duress Stress Disorder (PDSD). The physical and emotional damage caused by long-standing workplace bullying results from an accumulation of chronic, harmful, psychological assaults.

PDSD is not formally recognized as a mental health disorder by the American Psychiatric Association or any other global body of accreditation. It is, however, still undergoing research and is acknowledged by some mental health professionals as a more clinically correct picture of a target's suffering than PTSD. Proponents of this condition describe it as a predictable result of the many episodes of harassment and bullying upon the target. It is certainly well established that stress-related illnesses are caused not by one traumatic event, but by prolonged stress. To further the implications of PDSD, Namie and Namie describe three stages of stress:

1) The alarm stage, during which the body's self-defense systems are activated in a "fight or flight" posture

2) The resistance stage that maintains the body in an alert or standby posture

3) The exhaustion stage that consists of a full system breakdown, both physical and mental. This stage occurs after being on the defensive for a prolonged period of time.

We can again equate these stages with those found in the animal kingdom. A prey animal that senses danger will enter the alarm stage when the instinctive decision is made to fight the predator or attempt to escape from it. The animal enters the resistance stage when the immediate danger is no longer present, but the prey maintains a cautious alert stance. After a prolonged period of resistance, the prey animal enters the exhaustion stage; it can no longer feed or rest without fear, weakening it to the point that it finally breaks down and becomes the perfect target for a predator.

Prolonged bullying has the same effect on people. The target becomes so exhausted from a long period of alarm and resistance that he easily maintains the position of being preyed upon by a bullying predator. The workplace bully assaults the target until, as in the vernacular proverb, "resistance is futile." Although more research is needed on the Prolonged Duress Stress Disorder before it becomes a recognized, legitimate mental health disorder, the exhaustion of prolonged bullying exacts a terrible price from the target in all aspects of the target's life.

CASE STUDY: GAVIN

"I'm so tired of it all," said Gavin, a victim of long-term bullying. "I would hope that one day he gets back all that he gave me, times ten. I'm not God, and if he wants forgiveness, God will give it. But I won't. He made my life too miserable to be forgiven. Ha! I especially like that he calls himself a Christian who always talks about the Bible but doesn't live by it."

"The bosses who hide behind their power and authority are too protected by others who either share their ways or else don't care that people are being harmed. This will not get any better until someone at the top eradicates this abuse from his or her own office on down to individuals who are in charge of those of us who get the work done."

CASE STUDY: GAVIN

"But in all my life I've never seen a negative person transition themselves into a positive person, or seen a leopard change its spots. Unless you take into account the fact that the abuser was punished, he won't change."

In concluding this chapter, we must acknowledge one final price that the targets of workplace bullying face: a seemingly endless degree of rage, hate, frustration, and bitterness that is all too often acted out at home or even with a stranger who has more than ten items in the express checkout line at the supermarket. Helpless to vent their anger where it is deserved — at the bully and those who allow bullying in the workplace — targets act out their rage with others who are puzzled by their unprecedented behavior. They also turn their rage upon themselves, expressing it by substance abuse, suicide attempts, and intense feelings of self-hatred. Enduring both the effects of being bullied plus the burden of their hopeless hatred is a price that no one can stand for long and still maintain their physical and emotional health.

"If you care too much about what others think of you, then you will always be their prisoner."
—Lao Tzu

Chapter 5

Types of Workplace Bullying

"Most organizations have a serial bully. It never ceases to amaze me how one person's divisive, disordered, dysfunctional behavior can permeate the entire organization like a cancer."
— Tim Field

In the study of workplace bullying, Tim Field is acknowledged as one of the world's most prominent experts. Through the Field Foundation, Field and his brother, Michael, have amassed a huge amount of information about workplace bullying available to the public as well as forums where targets of bullying can share their stories of constant stress, surviving, and taking action against bullying. Field describes a bully as a person who:

- Has never learned to accept responsibility for their behavior

- Wants to enjoy the benefits of living in the adult world, but who is unable and unwilling to accept the responsibilities that are a prerequisite for being part of the adult world

- Abdicates and denies responsibility for their behavior and its consequences

- Is unable and unwilling to recognize the effect of their behavior on others

- Does not want to know of any other way of behaving

- Is unwilling to recognize that there could be better ways of behaving

After providing a general definition of workplace bullying, it is imperative to describe the many different types of bullying, the characteristics of bullying types, and why these types are adopted by workplace bullies. Bullying has nothing to do with managing; a bully may bear the title of "manager," but the real purpose of bullying is to hide the so-called manager's own inadequacy. Managers who bully, therefore, are acting in a manner than admits their inadequacy although they would deny any sense of feeling inadequate as a person or a manager. All types of bullying are meant to divert attention away from the inadequacies of the bully-manager; this is how they keep their jobs. Victimizing their targets and suavely justifying their actions to upper-level managers is a bully's way of having their secret discovered: that they are mortally fearful of being viewed as they truly are — weak and often incompetent. *Those who can, do. Those who cannot, bully.*

All the different types of bullies are individuals who are resentful, bitter, angry, and jealous of the abilities of others because they know they can never "measure up." In fact, bullies are driven primarily by jealousy and envy, especially of their targets. To make sure their targets do not surpass them in competency, bullies of all types must virtually destroy them. A bully's fear of being "discovered" often borders on paranoia. Since all of these feelings occur on a subconscious level, bullies truly believe in their worth and adequacy and refuse to consider otherwise. Since only feelings and behaviors that are acknowledged can be changed or relearned, it is very unlikely that any type of bully is capable of change.

Upper-level managers who are willing to consider the possibility that there is a bully in their workplace would see these warning signs:

- Staff turnovers

- Frequent absence

- Stress "breakdowns"

- Deaths by illness or suicide

- Early retirements

- Overuse of disciplinary procedures

- A large number of grievances by employees

- Frequent firing of employees

- The use of private security firms to "snoop" on employees after work hours

- Legal actions by employees

"It's so clear, a blind man could see it" is a popular vernacular term for a situation that is glaringly obvious, but denied or ignored by upper-level managers. But for sincere CEOs and others in positions of authority, once the existence of bullying is acknowledged, it becomes necessary to identify the type of bullying that is occurring within the walls of the workplace. Only then can superiors within the company take action to create a "zero tolerance" policy regarding workplace bullying. This chapter discusses the types of bullying as identified by the research of Tim Field and the team of Dr. Noa Davenport, Ruth Schwartz, and Gail Elliott.

Pressure Bullying occurs when some sort of stressor like a workplace inspection causes the behavior of a manager to deteriorate. This bully becomes temperamental, irritable, may shout and swear at subordinates, and make unreasonable demands upon targets. Once the stress has passed, the manager's behavior returns to "normal." This type of bullying becomes problematic when the stressed manager appears to select particular targets for his or her venting, knowing that they will not protest. Given that every workplace faces the stress of deadlines, high productivity, and excellence in job performance, pressure bullying also becomes problematic when it recurs with regularity.

Corporate Bullying occurs when a boss abuses one or more targets without fear of reprisal from either the law or upper-level management. These bullies fear nothing except the exposure of their own inadequacy. Examples of this type of bullying include:

- Forcing targets to work excessively long hours; anyone who objects is threatened with disciplinary action or termination. The targets capitulate because jobs in particular fields are sometimes scarce, and unemployment would be a financial and social disaster.

- Terminating targets of bullying who experience stress-related physical and/or emotional "meltdowns."

- Denial of annual leave or sick leave to which targets and any other employee is entitled as specified in their job descriptions. This action is punitive in nature, though the bully denies this truth if he or she is questioned by upper management. "I can't spare you right now; ask me again next month" is the bully's rationalization for this action.

- Snooping through a target's desk and personal property, reading the target's e-mail, listening to telephone conversations and other talk among employees, spying on the target after work hours and truly stalking the target in attempts to discover the target doing something inappropriate, contacting a target's customers without the target's knowledge and dropping hints to the customer that the target is a "problem child" within the organization, conducting illegal video surveillance of targets in the workplace, and requiring the target to supply confidential information about why the target was on sick leave.

- Documenting a stressed target as being "weak" and detrimental to the organization.

- Suggesting or overtly requiring other employees to disclose or even fabricate complaints about the target; threats of termination if they refuse.

- Insisting that the target give up an after-hours part-time job even though the target needs the extra income. Rationalizing this action by asserting that the target's work performance is suffering because of preoccupation with his or her part-time job.

Institutional Bullying shares many characteristics with corporate bullying. It occurs when all types of workplace bullying become a firmly entrenched part of an organization and is accepted by employees as well as midlevel and upper-level managers. Bullying becomes part of the company's way of life. Targets are moved to different work stations for no discernable or profitable reason; instead, they're moved to prevent employees from banding together against bullying. The targets suddenly find their long-term contracts with the company replaced with short-term contracts with fewer benefits; the clear implication by the bully is "accept this…or else." Targets' workloads are hopelessly increased and when they fail to meet deadlines they are disciplined or terminated. Roles and positions are changed; targets may find themselves no longer in charge of important projects and are demoted to unchallenging "busy work" with no real value to the company. Targets' career progressions are impeded; raises and promotions are denied without giving the targets a chance to respond. The message behind institutional bullying is that the bully rules with an iron fist and plays only by his rules. Those employees who do not like these conditions are invited to quit their jobs. Targets often try to survive being bullied in this manner for financial reasons, but they pay a high price in terms of physical and emotional stress.

Vicarious Bullying is a favorite tactic of the manipulative, sneaky, and suave bully. It is similar to individuals who enjoy dog or rooster fighting, except that this "game" is played with human beings. The bully subtly creates an environment or situation where two targets are pitted against each other in adversarial interactions and conflicts. The conflict may concern which target will receive a "prize" project, a raise, or a promotion. The bully is never overt about beginning the conflict; before they realize it, the targets find themselves to be gladiators in the bully's arena. Animal fighting is illegal in every American state, yet vicarious bullying is not only tolerated in some organizations, but is actively encouraged. Watching the combatants, the bully smiles with delight and thinks "may the best man win." In the bully's heart, he or she is a throwback to the decadent, cruel days of the Roman Empire when violent death was a form of entertainment. So too is the vicarious bully entertained by the stress and struggles of the targeted employees.

"My working conditions became so impossible that, for the first time in my life, I felt rage and despair. I have five children. To quit the job wasn't an option. I had no options except to grit my teeth and make it from one payday to the next."
— **Diana, a target of institutional bullying**

Serial Bullying can be identified when the source of all the dysfunction within an organization can be traced to one individual. According to Tim Field, this is the most common type of bullying. He refers to the serial bully as a "socialized psychopath" similar in nature to the narcissistic and antisocial personality disordered bullies. In the book *Snakes in Suits: When Psychopaths Go to Work*, Paul Babiak and Robert Hare describe the devastation that serial bullies inflict upon an individual target. Day by day, target by target, this bully lays waste to the physical and mental health of each employee that he or she picks to be the most current victim of his unrepentant cruelty. This is a bully who must have a target. When one target leaves the job or is terminated, the serial bully moves on to searching for the next target.

CASE STUDY: CHRIS

Chris is the legal counsel for a large, profitable corporation. As the business's attorney, one of his responsibilities is to examine complaints and grievances filed by employees against bosses or other employees.

"My job is to represent the company's best interest by determining if these grievances have merit and should be addressed, or whether they can be proven to be without merit. To make this determination, I need to interview the employee who filed the grievance, the person against whom the grievance was filed, and any witnesses who may have information about the nature and cause of the grievance. Of course, employees and employers will have disagreements that can usually be settled through our mediation program."

CASE STUDY: CHRIS

"I've been with the company for six years and am personally acquainted with higher management. The CEO wishes to be briefed on every grievance that, in my opinion, has merit.

"In the past year, I couldn't help but notice a trend; within that time frame one particular midlevel manager had 56 grievances filed against him. This is more than the complaints received about other managers combined. I found that not all these 56 grievances had legal merit, but the majority of them did constitute slander, libel, defamation, or harassment. Some of the grievances were resolved through mediation between this manager and the employee, but many are still unresolved and leave the company open to civil lawsuits.

"When I briefed the CEO about this overabundance of grievances against one individual, she said, 'Fifty-six people can't all be wrong or overreacting.' She inquired about my perception of the grievances and whether the manager's subordinates could be fabricating these complaints. I advised her that in my experience, people may lie about having money, fabulous vacations that never happened, or accomplishments in other jobs that are false. But 56 people have no reason to fabricate situations that have caused them extreme stress.

"With legal releases of information, we can obtain the medical and mental health records of the complainants to prove their job stress-related illnesses. Simply examining employees' time cards that document absences would tell us much. The CEO instructed me to conduct a discreet but large-scale evaluation of the subject of the grievances. By the sheer number of the grievances and their similarities in the alleged misconduct of the subject, I'm fairly certain of what I will discover. However, I still must remain impartial and open-minded."

"Lack of knowledge of, or unwillingness to recognize, or outright denial of the existence of the serial bully is the most common reason for an unsatisfactory outcome of a bullying case for both the employee and the employer."
— Tim Field

Field describes the characteristics and behavior of serial bullies as follows:

- Are convincing, practiced liars and when called to account, will make up anything spontaneously to fit their needs at the moment.

- Have a "Jekyll and Hyde" nature. They are vile, vicious, and vindictive in private, but innocent and charming in front of witnesses. No one can (or wants to) believe that this individual has a cruel nature; they are charming and convincing enough to deceive personnel and higher managers. The "Jekyll" side of this bully is an act; the "Hyde" side is the real person.

- Excel at deception and should never be underestimated in their capacity to deceive.

- Use of excessive charm and false sincerity and are always plausible and convincing when peers, superiors, or others are present, covering for their lack of empathy.

- Glib, shallow, and superficial with many fine words and lots of form, but always lacking in substance of character.

- Are possessed of an exceptional verbal ease and will outmaneuver most others in verbal interactions, especially during times of conflict.

- Are often described as smooth, slippery, slimy, ingratiating, fawning, toadying, obsequious, and sycophantic.

- Rely on mimicry, repetition, and regurgitation to convince others that he or she is a "normal" person, a tough, dynamic manager while pouring forth the accompanying jargon.

- Are unusually skilled in being able to anticipate what people want to hear and then saying it plausibly.

- Cannot be trusted or relied upon; fail to fulfill commitments.

- Have an arrested level of emotional development; their language and intellect may appear to be that of an adult, but the bully displays the emotional age of a small child.

- In work and personal relationships, they are unable to initiate or sustain emotional intimacy.

- Hold deep prejudices, but go to great lengths to prevent this from being known.

- Are opinionated, arrogant, have audacity and a sense of entitlement, invulnerability, and invincibility.

- Have a compulsive need to control what everyone else does, thinks, or believes.

- Have a compulsive need to criticize and devalue others; they refuse to value, praise, or acknowledge the achievements of others.

- Refuse to give straight answers; they exaggerate facts and evade honest accountability.

- Undermine and destroy anyone whom they perceive as an adversary, a potential threat, or those who can see through their "Jekyll" mask.

- Adept at creating conflict between those who would

otherwise collaborate in revealing incriminating information about them.

- Quickly discredit and neutralize anyone who can speak knowledgeably about antisocial or sociopathic behaviors.

- Pursuit of vendettas against anyone who dares to hold them accountable and are contemptuous of the damage they cause others with these vendettas.

- Quickly belittle, undermine, denigrate, and discredit anyone who calls, or attempts to call, this bully to account for his or her actions.

- Highly manipulative of other people's perceptions and emotions.

- Gain gratification from denying people what they are entitled to.

- When called upon to address the needs and concerns of others, they respond with impatience, irritability, and aggression.

- Are arrogant, haughty, high-handed, selfish, mean-spirited, petty, officious know-it-alls, and emotional parasitic vampires. They are always "takers" rather than "givers."

- Have overwhelming needs to be seen as wonderful, kind, caring, and compassionate.

- Are "spiritually dead" although they may profess some religious beliefs.

- They are convinced of their superiority to others and have overbearing beliefs in their qualities of leadership.

- Constantly impose upon others a false reality made up of their own distortions and fabrications.

With this very lengthy and detailed description of serial bullies, Field makes it clear that these are extremely dangerous individuals that relentlessly and systematically destroy their targets in the workplace. The fact that they lack insight into their behavior makes them all the more dangerous for the targets and for the organization. It is well to note that more suicides and incidents of workplace violence occur when serial bullying or mob bullying are present. Targets of serial bullies often feel that they have run out of both options and the strength to endure. They are so demoralized and exhausted that suicide seems the most plausible course of action — the final chapter in the history of a bully's target. In the vernacular, "their get-up-and-go just got-up-and-went." With no champion among coworkers or upper-level managers, targets of serial bullies believe that no one knows, or wants to know, what they are being subjected to on a daily basis. Partly in despair and party for retribution, targets commit suicide and make sure that the world knows that their deaths are on their bullies' heads; their blood is on the hands of the upper-level managers who let it all happen.

> *"They were not listening,*
> *They did not know how;*
> *Perhaps they'll listen now."*
> **Don McLean**
> **"Vincent"**

Serial bullies are oblivious to their crassness and have permanently switched off their morals and ethics, if indeed they ever had any. The prisons of the world are filled with people who share these characteristics of serial bullies. The only difference between criminals and serial bullies is that criminals are blatantly unsocialized, where serial "white-collar" bullies manage to keep their behavior within the confines of the law. The targets of a serial bully feel precisely as the victim of a sexual predator feels; violated, helpless, furious, shocked, and thoroughly demoralized. If Field and other experts on bullying and sociopathic behavior are correct, then there is no hope that this bully can be rehabilitated. Their pervasive pathology is "hard-wired" into them; as the snake in the earlier parable said to the frog, "I can't help it. It's my nature." Serial bullies regard mediation as appeasement for the upper-level managers but having no real value. Although they give the impression of being sincere and conciliatory, privately they merely continue bullying. Since sociopathic serial bullies take no responsibility for their actions, they will not learn from their mistakes even if they are discovered and punished. The only way for upper-level management to deal with a serial bully, according to Field, is immediate dismissal for the sake of the targets and the organization as a whole. The lesson we must learn, says Field, is that we do not appease aggressors.

Dr. Stanton Samenow is a world-renowned expert in criminology, having pioneered this forensic behavioral field in 1984 with the publication of his seminal work, *Inside the Criminal Mind.* Samenow has continued to research and publish in the field of criminology and the antisocial, or sociopathic, personality. His 1998 publication *Straight Talk About Criminals* describes the antisocial individual who does not commit crimes but still victimizes others. He characterized these individuals as those who shamelessly and without conscience use others to their own advantage. Due to the fact that they have no empathy for others, they single-mindedly pursue their objectives with no remorse for the harm that they cause. If these individuals are confronted about their antisocial behavior they become indignant and self-righteous while blaming their victim(s) for their own misery. In *Inside the Criminal Mind*, Samenow directly relates sociopathic thinking with the workplace, making the point that these individuals misuse their authority at work in a subtle manner. With a criminal-thinking manager steering the boat, Samenow notes that employee morale deteriorates. In time, employees are discouraged to the point that they no longer propose innovative ideas and solutions that could financially benefit the company.

CASE STUDY: RUTH

Even before she accepted a new job, Ruth had heard rumors about the man who would be her boss, Scott. Ruth was new to the area and did not know anyone at the company well. But when she interviewed for the job, she had an uneasy feeling that some of the employees were indirectly warning her about Scott. Sure that she was mistaken, Ruth accepted the job and found Scott to be very welcoming and pleasant.

"I've never misjudged anyone as badly as I misjudged Scott. I always thought I was a pretty good judge of character, but I was incredibly wrong about Scott. I only had an entry-level position in the office, but one of my project managers, Clark, seemed very unhappy all the time. I didn't talk to him about things that were not of my business, but I could tell that he seemed really depressed at times and anxious at other times. I know he had a lot of headaches because he had a big bottle of medicine on his desk and he rubbed his head a lot. Nearly every day, Scott called Clark into his office and shut the door. When Clark came out, he was usually pale, shaking, and looked very angry.

"A few weeks later, Clark went on a two-week sick leave. On the day he got back, Scott fired him for poor work performance. We had a farewell party

CASE STUDY: RUTH

for him, which made Scott mad, but we did it anyway. Then Clark told us that he was on sick leave because of stress-related bleeding ulcers.

"After Clark left, things were pretty calm and quiet for a while. Then Scott started in on me. I was still on my probationary period, so his constant criticism made me really afraid about being fired. I couldn't do anything right to please Scott. Every day he'd find something to pick at me about. One day he called me "lazy" and when I got a little angry, he said I needed to develop more self control. I began to see Scott as the most arrogant, obnoxious person I've ever met. He was better than everyone else; once he even said, 'I should be running this company so I could get rid of all the deadbeats.'"

"He must have read on my job application form that I was a Mormon because he made it a point to tell me that the LDS church was a cult and that I should 'come back to Jesus.' I told him that I'd never left Jesus to begin with. It made him really angry when I stood up for myself, and he just got worse. One month my productivity was the highest in the office, and he never even mentioned it at our next staff meeting. He couldn't stand to see me do anything well.

"Several of us liked to play Spades during our lunch break, and Scott wrote us up for gambling at work. Any idiot knows that Spades is just a card game, not gambling. I know he looked through my desk on read my e-mails after work because things weren't where I left them. One of my coworkers told me that Scott told her that I was 'trouble' and she should stay away from me. But if Scott's own boss ever showed up in our workplace, Scott was as sweet as can be, telling the boss what good work we do.

"Then he asked the boss if he could speak to him privately in his office. Maybe I'm just paranoid, but I saw the boss glance over at me, so they must have been talking about me. Scott had this real earnest look on his face that made me sick. When he told me that he was denying my annual leave because I hadn't finished a project, I told him that my coworker had volunteered to finish the project so I could go to my family reunion. He said no, that project was assigned to me and only I was to work on it.

"I filed a grievance against him, and that settled him down for a little while,

CASE STUDY: RUTH

but not for long. He must have really wanted to punish me for filing the grievance, because everything got worse. He was at me all day, every day. I was just exhausted. I couldn't stop crying and I didn't give a damn about anything. I just stayed at home by myself instead of being with my friends. I felt tired all the time and slept all weekend. I went to my doctor who diagnosed me with irritable bowel syndrome and high blood pressure. He said this was unusual for someone that was only 25 and then he asked about my stress level. I burst into tears and told him the whole story. He got me an appointment for therapy, which has helped a lot. But I'm quitting that job.

"Putting up with Scott isn't worth it. I don't care if I'm broke and have to live under a bridge. I just can't take him anymore. I don't know how Clark put up with Scott for so long. I didn't even make it for six months. Now he'll just find another sucker."

It is clear from Ruth's story that serial bullies use criticism and humiliation not to address shortfalls in a target's job performance as they claim, but to control and subjugate the target. Ruth was new on the job, young, and female; these are all seen as vulnerabilities to a male serial bully. After Clark was fired, Scott had a "cooling off" period until he located Ruth, yet another target. Ruth chose to quit her job rather than endure further bullying, but many targets cannot financially afford to quit, even though they desperately wish for freedom from the bully. The serial bully, of course, knows this; he or she can look forward to many days of torturing the target who is little more than a hostage. With the serial bully, the beat always goes on. Only the song changes, not the musicians.

Mob Bullying

"If one person tells you that you're an elephant, you can blow if off.
But if several people say the same thing, you'd better go join a circus."
— A Therapist's Proverb

In their landmark work, *Mobbing: Emotional Abuse in the Workplace*, Davenport, Schwartz, and Elliott describe the target of mob workplace bullying as being "driven beyond endurance." As traumatic as it is to be bullied by a particular bully in the workplace, being mob bullied is by far the most devastating form of bullying that can be inflicted upon a targeted employee.

Victims of mob bullying at work are numbered in the *millions*. Individual targets are isolated and made to feel, by their bullies, that they are the problem; they are unique and no one else suffers as they do. It is, according to the bullies, the fault of the target for bringing about his or her downfall in the workplace. This is a vicious lie and manipulation by the mob bullies; these predatory individuals who appear to be without conscience make certain that their target becomes so demoralized that he or she eventually accepts this lie without question. The reality is that targets of mob bullying are usually good job performers, well qualified for their tasks, and had contributed their abilities to an organization for several years. Davenport et al. cite three reasons why mob bullying persists in the workplace:

1) Mobbing behavior is ignored, tolerated, misinterpreted, or instigated by the organization's upper-level management.

2) Mobbing has not yet been classified as a behavior that is clearly different from sexual harassment and/or discrimination.

3) Targets of mobbing become worn down, burned out, destroyed, and exhausted. After prolonged mobbing, targets feel incapable of defending themselves.

This section follows one story of a mob-bullied individual who experienced the full gamut of this devastating type of bullying.

CASE STUDY: SIOBHAN PART 1

Siobhan is a 49-year-old Caucasian woman who has worked for the same organization for fifteen years. She is married to a man who works for the same company; when one was transferred to a different location, the other was always allowed to follow.

Siobhan had always received excellent performance reports, but she has a history of clinical major depression and takes antidepressive medication that has been of great benefit to her. Siobhan is bright, well qualified, good at her work, and has always been liked by her coworkers. She has been a midlevel manager for the past ten years.

Two years ago, Siobhan and her husband were transferred to a new location with the same company. Her duties included the overall supervision of her work station and eight subordinates of varying skill levels. Siobhan met with her new immediate supervisor, the supervisor of the division, and the organization's top executive and found them friendly, likeable, and pleasant. She got the same feelings about her subordinates, and looked forward to a pleasant working environment. In her first meeting with her immediate supervisor, she was asked about possible personal factors that might impede her job performance. Siobhan felt that her supervisor was trustworthy, so she discussed her history of depression, making the point that according to her physician, she was in full, sustained remission from any symptoms of depression and would likely discontinue her medication in a few months. From that day forward, Siobhan began to have difficulties in her workplace.

The term "to mob" means to crowd about, attack or annoy others. Mobs are generally thought of as unruly crowds with ill intentions towards another person or persons. The study of mobbing in the workplace outside the U.S. was initiated in the 1980s by Dr. Heinz Leymann in Sweden, and then in Germany. (Cited in Cavaiola and Lavender) Leymann discovered in his research that certain individuals, whom we now call targets, were labeled as "difficult" people in the workplace by managers. What he discovered were workplaces that created the circumstances that labeled these employees as "difficult"; the organization then created further reasons for firing these employees. Leymann identified this behavior as mobbing.

Leymann published his first academic report on the mobbing phenomenon in 1984's *Mobbing: Psychoterror at the Workplace and How You Can Defend Yourself* (cited in Davenport et al.). He subsequently published more than 60 articles and books on the subject of mobbing. In the next few years, similar studies were conducted (and are still ongoing) in Norway, Finland, the UK, Ireland, Switzerland, Austria, Hungary, Italy, France, Australia, New Zealand, Japan, and South Africa.

In 1976, Dr. Carroll Brodsky wrote *The Harassed Worker* (cited in Davenport et al.) based upon complaints filed with the California Workers' Compensation Appeals Board and the Nevada Industrial Commission. Brodsky noted that these claims were based upon employees' statements that they were unable to work because of the psychological effects of being ill-treated by employers or coworkers. Independent of each other, Brodsky and Leymann both noted that the target of mobbing is forced into a helpless, defenseless position that persists continuously over a prolonged period of time.

In the ensuing years, research on mobbing in the workplace has virtually exploded in the U.S. with accompanying publications by numerous academic experts. Mob bullying is generally defined as behavior that the target perceives to be unwarranted, unreasonable, excessive, or a violation of human rights. The media has been shining the spotlight on mobbing; in November 1998, Oprah Winfrey's show focused on bullying bosses who often lead others into the fray of targeting an individual employee. To date, thousands of Web sites are dedicated to workplace bullying and mob bullying in particular.

"I thought I was alone, that no one else ever experienced anything like what was done to me. I figured out that I was being ganged up on, but I didn't know the term "mobbing" and certainly never knew that this was not just a national problem, but an international problem."
— Siobhan

Davenport et al. describe mobbing as an emotional assault. Charting the course of mob bullying, it begins with disrespectful and harmful actions toward the target, escalating into abusive and terrorizing behavior, and culminates when the target is reduced to unbearable emotional distress, physical illness, and complete social misery. The target often uses sick leave to escape the relentless torment, becoming depressed and accident-prone due to lack of concentration. The target may eventually resign or retire early even though he or she cannot financially afford to do so. If not, the target will be finally terminated and expelled from the workplace. All too often, the target is so filled with shame and humiliation after being mobbed that suicide results from the psychoterror that he or she was subjected to on a daily basis. Although this is a tragic outcome for the target's friends and family, for the target at least, there will be no more tears. The danger to the target of mobbing cannot be overemphasized.

"I really don't know how I survived those eighteen months. I almost didn't; suicide was always on my mind and once I made an attempt. But somehow I dragged myself into that place every day with as much dignity as I could muster. I threw up every morning in the parking lot. May God damn them for what they did to me."
— Siobhan

Dr. Heinz Leymann identified 45 mobbing behaviors and classified them into five different categories:

- Impact on self-expression and communication

- Attacks on the target's social relations and interactions at work

- Attacks on the target's reputation

- Attacks on the quality of the target's profession and life situations

- Direct attacks on the target's health

Leymann's list and typologies can be found in the appendix of this book, and is a must-read for academic researchers and targets of mobbing. Any of these behaviors occurring alone and in an isolated incident would certainly be inappropriate; mobbing occurs when most, if not all, of these actions happen daily, on a prolonged basis, and by more than one person. Leymann also describes five distinct phases of mobbing — each one clearly escalating into the next:

Conflict

↓

Aggressive acts

↓

Management involvement

↓

Branding as "difficult" or "mentally ill"

↓

Expulsion from the workplace

Conflicts with a boss or coworker are not unusual in the workplace; wherever people work in close quarters on a daily basis, conflicts are bound to occur and in healthy workplaces are quickly and amicably resolved. Conflicts are not mobbing behaviors but they are the first step toward mobbing. As the progression continues, aggressive acts such as psychological assaults begin to occur toward an employee who will eventually become a mobbing target. Upper-level management personnel have a choice to make as the phases continue; they can either step in and call a halt to the developing hostilities or they can join the mob by beginning the isolation and expulsion process. Leymann describes phase four as crucial in the development of mobbing; the now clearly identified target is labeled as a difficult or mentally ill employee, serving only to seriously escalate the mobbing. This phase almost always leads to the last phase of expulsion of the target from the workplace.

CASE STUDY: SIOBHAN PART 2

Using Leymann's five phases of mobbing, Siobhan's story becomes clearer:

Conflict: In personality style with subordinates

Aggressive Acts: Subordinates who disliked Siobhan's leadership style complained about her to the immediate supervisor. Siobhan was not allowed to express her side of the story. She was given letters of counseling and verbal warnings. The immediate supervisor and Siobhan's subordinates meet with the higher supervisor about Siobhan's leadership style. Immediate supervisor tells subordinates not to talk with Siobhan without a "witness." Subordinates begin to keep a file on everything Siobhan does that they don't like. Both supervisors are aware of — or perhaps initiated — the file.

CASE STUDY: SIOBHAN PART 2

Management Involvement: The top-level manager of the company believes all that is said about Siobhan without personally checking the facts. Siobhan is removed from her workplace, stripped of her leadership position and responsibilities, physically isolated from other company workers, and is given no work to perform. Her keys are taken and she is not allowed to speak with other coworkers or former clients. Siobhan is almost daily reprimanded for petty or false misdeeds and severely disciplined for one incident that was embellished and contained false accusations by her subordinates. All levels of management began to create a "paper trail" that would serve as reasons for Siobhan's expulsion. Siobhan is notified of official action to be taken against her to ensure her expulsion.

Branded as Difficult or Mentally Ill: In relation to the mobbing, Siobhan suffers another episode of major depression. To cope, she begins to drink alcohol to excess in secret. Siobhan is preoccupied with thoughts of suicide and makes one unsuccessful attempt, also in secret. She remains in total isolation from the rest of the company workers. Siobhan is subjected to a mental evaluation by the company's hand-picked "hired gun" psychiatrist, who brands her as mentally unstable and recommends her expulsion. Siobhan fights back by demanding a termination hearing; every member of the mobbing group gives false or misleading information about her. Siobhan loses the hearing.

Expulsion: Siobhan is terminated from her job. On her last day, not one person tells her goodbye; she became invisible. Siobhan continues to experience depression, stress-related illnesses, and alcohol abuse. On her own, she seeks treatment for these conditions. The effects of having been mob bullied continue to affect her self-esteem to the present day.

CASE STUDY: SIOBHAN PART 2

Siobhan, in her own words:

"The person responsible for actually organizing the attacks by my subordinates, immediate supervisor, and upper-level manager into mob bullying was my supervisor's supervisor. I've heard it said that evil kills the spirits of others, and that's what this man did to me. He is a sick, sick bastard. The others were only too glad to go along with him because they didn't want him to target them. He ruled our workplace by terror, and it wasn't just me he did it to, although my situation was the worst. He wasn't a leader; he was the instigator of a mob of jackals that were too afraid of him to say, 'No, I won't be a part of this.' Besides, the rest of them enjoyed what they did to me because they thought, in their self-righteous way, that I deserved what I got simply because I did things differently than they did.

"There was no room for diversity in that accursed workplace. Once I was targeted, the outcome was preordained; it was simply a matter of when and how I would be forced out. They did it in the cruelest ways possible and I just melted down and did things to hurt myself like attempt suicide and drink too much. I fantasized about killing them slowly and painfully over and over again; I felt that kind of rage toward them. Why did this happen? I wasn't bothering anyone by being different in personality style, and the quality of my work, so said my clients, was always good.

"This second-level supervisor once told me that he'd like to kick my father's ass for committing suicide when my father was terminally ill. Yeah, as if he could! My father was a better man at 80 that he will ever be, and my father died because he loved his kids enough to spare them from his lingering death. This same sick bastard also said that 'when this is all over,' meaning my expulsion, 'we should go out and drink beer. You drink beer don't you?' Are you kidding me? Were we supposed to be buddies or some warped thing? By that time I had a serious alcohol abuse problem, and he wants to drink beer with me. Right. I'm a Christian person and I believe that where mercy is shown, mercy is given. But I will hate these people for the rest of my life and wish them nothing but ill. I know that's un-Christian thinking, but God will just have to judge me for it. But to be honest, I hate myself more than I hate them because for a long, long time I believed what they said about me. I think I still do."

In "bully-think," there is strength in numbers. Seeing that the goal of the bully is to force the target's expulsion, the bully figures that this will be easier to accomplish if he recruits a number of like-minded subordinates who will do his will with relish, especially if they dislike the vulnerable target in some way. Anyone could become the target of a serial bully who also instigates mob bullying, but there are certain characteristics that make an employee more likely to be picked as a target as in Siobhan's story. According to Davenport et al., anyone can become the target of mob bullying regardless of their age, devotion to the mission of the company, creativity, experience, sense of responsibility, ability to organize tasks, and their degree of self-initiation at work. Mobbing instigators are almost always serial bullies who see an opportunity to "lead" a pack of already hungry predators into the emotional and physical annihilation of the target. Using a parody of John Donne's famous work, targets should not send to know for whom the bullying bell tolls; it tolls for just about anybody who is vulnerable.

> *"They were not listening,*
> *they're not listening still —*
> *Perhaps they never will."*
> **— Don McLean**
> **"Vincent"**

The psychology of mob bullying is baffling, and as yet no definitive research exists that clarifies the psyche of these bullies who all act in concert to willfully and happily destroy another person. Some theories of the psychological aspects of mob bullying suggest that these are people who are indifferent to the pain of others, have a grandiose and inflated sense of self, are in desperate need to control and exercise power over others simply because they can, and suffer a deep-seated and hidden feeling of fear and inadequacy. Perhaps the answer lies within the personality disorders discussed in a previous chapter. Experts in the field have put forward a number of theories about the psychology of mob bullies:

- They are compelled to force others to adapt to group norms; differences in personality work style are not tolerated.

- They destroy others because they like animosity; those they do not like must be expelled from their midst.

- They enjoy what they do. They gain sadistic pleasure in seeing and creating the suffering of others.

- Bullying bosses who recruit willing sycophants feel that because of their position, they have a right to do what they do.

- Their fragile egos are somehow threatened by the target. To restore their twisted ego structure, they must destroy that threat by any means necessary.

- The organizational structure is conducive to mobbing through the indifference, ignorance, or gullibility of a top manager. Thus, the organization is ineffectively managed by a weak top manager who believes everything he is told about the target; he makes no effort to determine the facts on his own. The mob has a free rein to do as they please to whomever they please.

Early psychiatric pioneer Alfred Adler, a contemporary of Freud and Jung, originated the concept of social interest. Decades before personality disorder theories were standardized, Adler speculated that individuals who had no empathy with others, no remorse for their misdeeds toward others, and lack involvement in their community are devoid of the social interest that can be found in emotionally healthy individuals. Applying Adler's theory to mob bullies, it could be hypothesized that these bullies care nothing for the effects of their actions on not just the target, but also on the workplace community as a whole. When someone in the workplace becomes the target of mobbing, other employees become fearful, confused, annoyed, and develop feelings of guilt for not attempting to intervene on the target's behalf. The social structure of the workplace is severely disrupted and work production and performance overall decreases, a fact that is either missed or dismissed by the top manager. In particular, the lead mobber's actions are misconstrued by gullible top managers as being loyal to the company and devoted to acting in its best interest by ridding the organization of a mentally unstable and problematic employee. For mobs, other people are disposable.

For other examples of mobbing, we can look into world history. One person, acting alone, could never have achieved the destruction and death of so many targets: Genghis Khan, Idi Amin, Joseph Stalin, Adolf Hitler, and Saddam Hussein are but a few examples of how serial bullies recruit willing or fearful mobs. If Charles Manson had not had the charisma, intelligence, and lack of social interest that he displayed all his life in the manipulation of others, at least seven innocent targets might be alive today. More than 900 people committed mass suicide at the command of Jim Jones. Those who resisted Jones' order to die were executed by his hardcore followers. Mob instigators do not allow dissention or disobedience.

"The purpose of our existence is to help other human beings.
If we cannot do that, the least we can do is not hurt them."
– The Dalai Lama

In summary, Davenport et al. identified ten key factors of the mob bullying syndrome; the emotional and physical effects suffered by the target are a direct result of these factors:

- Assaults upon the dignity, integrity, credibility, and professional competence of the target.

- Negative, humiliating, intimidating, abusive, malevolent, and controlling communication by the mob to the target.

- The mob is committed either directly or indirectly to destroying the target in either subtle or blatantly obvious ways.

- Mobbing is perpetrated by several staff members — "vulturing."

- Mobbing occurs in a continual, multiple, and systematic fashion over time.

- The mobbers portray the target as being at fault.

- Mobbing is designed to discredit, confuse, intimidate, isolate, and force the target into submission.

- Mobbing is committed with the intent of bringing about the expulsion of the target from the company.

- Mobbers misrepresent the expulsion of the target from the workplace as being the target's own choice.

- Mob bullying is not recognized, misinterpreted, ignored, tolerated, encouraged, or instigated by top-level managers.

Bullying in the Military: A Unique Problem

Every day, members of the U.S. Armed Forces risk their lives to preserve, protect, and defend our Constitution. All military personnel, officers and enlisted, take a solemn oath to fulfill their duty and obey the officers appointed over them. These men and women who wear the uniform of their service branch and their country readily agree to give their lives in the performance of their duty. No one joins the military and takes this oath without knowing that someday they may be required to engage in combat "against all enemies, foreign and domestic" in a hostile environment and in stark living conditions for a prolonged period of time.

Military commanders have a unique power that no other boss or supervisor has; they can order a subordinate to perform tasks. To be legal under the Uniform Code of Military Justice, an order must be clearly understood by the subordinate and given directly to him or her rather than through a third party or on paper and e-mails. Disobeying a legal order is a extremely serious offense and is harshly punished from monetary fines to time in confinement facilities, to receiving a "bad conduct" discharge, all depending upon the nature of the disobedience.

Absolute power corrupts absolutely, so the saying goes. Military commanders do not have absolute power over their subordinates, but frighteningly close to it. When setting policies, initiating tasks, and disciplining subordinates for any purpose, the reasoning behind a commander's authority is to "maintain good order and discipline" among the troops; this phrase is incredibly well known among both commanders and their subordinates. Yet this concept can be, and often is, misused by some commanders as a rationale for behavior that is clearly bullying. Commanders who bully their target subordinates hide behind classifying the bullying as being necessary to maintain good order and discipline. Taking a closer look at a commander's power and authority yields a revelation that military commanders bully in exactly the same way as other bullies. So rarely are they questioned about their actions; bullied subordinates do have grievance procedures, but using these procedures, which are primarily internal, do not often result in any type of change in the bully's behavior; the military protects its own.

There are several remedies for bullied subordinates: (1) a grievance filed with the Equal Opportunity office in cases of discrimination; (2) requesting an investigation to the on-base Inspector General; and (3) going outside the system and filing a complaint with a subordinate's local congressman. These three remedies seldom result in change and commanders have a long memory when it comes to writing performance reports for subordinates. Even though a military member can prove a clear case of bullying, chances are that the commander's actions will be written off as maintaining good order and discipline while discrediting the reputation of the member and intimidating him or her through the commander's ability to ruin careers through bad performance reports.

CASE STUDY: DEVON

"The truth is, we are the backbone of the military," said Devon, an enlisted senior Technical Sergeant. "Just like those officers who supervise us, we are dedicated to doing the best job we can to help accomplish the mission. We have just as much equity in our positions and professionalism as those who govern us, even if some of the commanders don't adhere to our motto of 'Integrity First, Service for Others, and Excellence in All We Do.'"

CASE STUDY: DEVON

"I've had a couple of commanders that made my life hell. They would have had no problem with tossing my long career out the window for the slightest infractions of rules. I'm not a poster child for perfection, but they sure thought they were. You're stuck with the commander you work for at any military base. And because all enlisted personnel sign on for 4-6 years, it's not like being a civilian where you can walk out the door anytime. You're just plain stuck and have to put up with being harassed, insulted, humiliated, and nagged.

"A commander's word is like God. They can write anything off as being for good order and discipline and no one will question their actions unless they punch you in the face or something. Being harassed by commanders happens more often that you think; the public just doesn't hear about it. Besides, if we talk about being abused, it would bring unwanted attention to their sick personality traits and question their abilities to manage and lead others. Nobody seems to want to go there. I have worked for and observed several of these people; I've seen them in action against me and other subordinates. One reason they do this is because of bigotry; another reason is that they're sick enough to use their authority to destroy rather than create. They think they are superior to us; our feelings and our careers aren't worth a second thought. We enlisted personnel and the junior officers bear the brunt of their hatred, or their upbringing or their convictions, and we have to adapt to keep from being completely beaten down.

"Once one of these commander picks someone to abuse, there's no changing their minds or stopping their actions. All the so-called remedies like going to the Inspector General or filing a congressional complaint are just bullshit. It doesn't help, but it looks good. A lot of people leave after their term is up, or ask to be reassigned to another base, or cross-train into a new career field to get away from these idiots who make our lives miserable. I've seen suicides that were written as the victim being mentally unstable. I've seen people just lose it from being stressed and harassed all the time. I've seen divorces and alcohol abuse and depression. What's funny is that the 'brass' is always trying to figure out why so many officers and enlisted personnel leave the military and why so many suicides occur as result of work stress. If they'd listen to us for a change, they'd know the answer."

Workplace bullying in the military can consist of:

- Commanders and supervisors assigning difficult tasks that are due within an unreasonably short period of time.

- Continually assigning unpleasant duties to the target when such duties are frequently rotated among personnel.

- Denying the target's request for leave for no just cause; citing the reason as being "for good order and discipline" and the needs of the workplace mission.

- Being constantly criticized for their work, their appearance, and their military bearing.

- Singling out targeted personnel for abusive treatment, knowing that they can get away with it because of their positions of power and authority.

- Writing unwarranted poor performance reports that will prevent the target from being promoted; knowing that more than one "do not promote" report will result in the target being involuntarily discharged.

- Barraging the target with frequent out of proportion disciplinary actions, e.g., letters of counseling, letters of reprimand, poor performance reports, removal from positions of leadership, assigning extra duty to enlisted personnel, confinement to the base, initiating serious nonjudicial punishments through Article 15 of the Uniform Code of Military Justice, and initiating court-martial proceedings against a subordinate. Any of these actions could result in the target's involuntary separation from the service with an other than honorable discharge, which precludes them from ever being hired for a government job, and many civilian jobs.

- Verbally and/or emotionally abusing targets under the auspices of maintaining good order and discipline.

- Being mob bullied by a target's full chain of command, from the base commander down to midlevel workplace supervisors and coworkers.

- Being physically isolated from coworkers and receiving "no contact" orders to prevent the target from talking with other workplace personnel about their situation.

- Manipulating and intimidating troops who are supportive of the target into making defamatory and/or misleading statements about the target for use in disciplinary actions.

- Issuing illegal orders in writing or through another person, and then punishing the target who does not obey the order, and questions its legality.

- Denying a target an upgraded security clearance without just cause, preventing the target from being promoted.

- Failure to adhere to the Department of Defense's regulations on the prevention of suicide and/or workplace violence.

- Ignoring the military's policy of "praising in public, criticizing in private," embarrassing the target among his or her peers.

- Refusal to endorse a deserved medal for the target's "going above and beyond" the call of duty or performing in an exemplary manner.

- Disregarding and ridiculing the target's legitimate stress-related illness and forcing him or her to remain on duty despite a physician's recommendation.

"I raised my right hand and took the oath before God and the American flag, and I meant it. But this kind of treatment isn't what I signed on for. I never thought I would be defending myself against my own commander rather than against a foreign enemy."
— **Author**

The exact number of active duty military personnel in each branch of service who attempt or complete suicide is not released to the public except possibly under the Freedom of Information Act. When a military suicide does occur, it is regarded as a "sentinel event" that is investigated by an appointed team from other military bases.

CASE STUDY: OLIVIA

"I never even knew this patient and didn't know he existed until the day he died," said Olivia, a senior Major and chief of a mental health clinic. "He was being seen by another psychotherapist, my subordinate, and his record indicates that he did have some significant mental health issues."

"Our squadron's policy is for clinic chiefs to be informed about possibly suicidal or homicidal personnel. Two of my subordinates knew that this airman's life was in danger and never bothered to tell me because they and senior personnel were mob bullying me to an unbearable degree. When the airman committed suicide, these two subordinates, my flight commander, my squadron commander, and even the medical group commander blamed me. On their say-so, without even talking directly to me, the investigator's report indicated that I was at fault for failing to provide good leadership and supervision of my subordinates. I was to blame for this young man's death, and I didn't even know, because I wasn't informed, that he was being seen in our clinic."

CASE STUDY: OLIVIA

"You can't imagine how that made me feel. Just because I had a different, less formal personality style than my subordinates, they completely disrespected me. One of them failed to show up for work because he hadn't slept well. He didn't even call me to ask for permission, which he knew I would have given. I could have walloped these two for many things but I didn't because I knew they would bitch to the flight commander and she'd take their side. But being blamed for this airman's death pushed me over the edge.

"I just lost it. I locked myself in my office and cried my heart out. I wouldn't answer the phone or knocks at the door; I didn't want my clinic to see me like that. I opened the door when the squadron commander ordered me to. Instead of being concerned and supportive, he sent me to the VA clinic for an emergency mental health evaluation just to cover his ass and make sure I didn't harm myself and blame it on him. Stuff doesn't just happen in the military; someone always has to be blamed. This time it was me. Although logically I know I was not the cause of this airman's death, emotionally I still think I was."

Bullying military commanders are very difficult to depose. Using Olivia's case as an example, she was later medically retired from the military due to severe major depression caused primarily due to being relentlessly mob bullied. Her medical group commander, a Colonel, took voluntary retirement. Her squadron commander, a Lt. Col., was passed over for promotion and sent to another base in a noncommander position. Her flight commander was also not promoted for the second time and was separated from the service. One of her subordinates separated due to pregnancy and the other was transferred to another base. These changes were not, standing alone, results from Olivia's case. Women are released from service, if they wish, due to pregnancy. Olivia's other mobbing subordinate was sent to a much smaller base, but in the state, that was his home. Olivia's flight commander was passed over for promotion for the second time and she was separated as a result. Olivia's medical group commander and squadron commander had so many complaints filed against them, by subordinate personnel with the Inspector General and congressmen, that the "brass" decided it was time that they moved on. Olivia received a report from the Inspector General, mostly redacted, that contained this information.

Military spouses have many difficult issues, especially if they live in base housing, at no charge, instead of off base. While the talk of free housing, medical and dental care, and commissary privileges often sparks controversy, there is a "downside" to being the spouse or children of a military member that civilians do not understand, and that come perilously close to bullying as the following vignette illustrates:

CASE STUDY: LISA

"There are some things that have annoyed me that have stuck in my mind," wrote Lisa, the wife of a senior sergeant. "Gary and I were in an argument outside by our car in the parking lot of the enlisted club. This was in the first year of our marriage. Some security cops came by and asked Gary what was going on. I 'went off' and was putting my two cents' worth in and again they spoke only to Gary, telling him to control his wife and saying that I did not understand what it was to be a military wife. It was like I was invisible, and extremely rude. Unless you're active duty, you may as well not exist unless you commit a crime."

"The other incident happened when we lived on base and it was a brutal winter. Gary was deployed to Oman during Desert Storm. I received three tickets from the security cops in just one month for leaving my outside lights on. I was told that I was wasting government money and that my husband could get in serious trouble over this. I was alone with a small child. I'm British and in a strange land. I left the lights on for our safety, not because I was wasteful. It's hard to believe that my husband, defending his country

CASE STUDY: LISA

during wartime, would be disciplined because I was nervous and left the lights on. Gary is ruled by the military, and the families are too. If we don't follow the rules about cutting and edging our lawn or shoveling snow within so many hours, we could lose our base housing. The active duty members are responsible for the actions of their family, and that doesn't seem right when Gary wasn't even there! Like I said, I'm invisible."

Civilian targets of workplace bullying have remedies that military members do not. Unless the bully physically touches the military target in a sexual or violent manner, senior-ranking commanders are largely untouchable for any civil tort action against them in local or federal court. Defamation, wrongful termination, and constructive discharge — all civilian court actions — are not punishable offenses under the Uniform Code of Military Justice. Active duty personnel have no legal remedies for these actions by a commander and have no protected status. There is no precedent regarding active duty members suing active duty commanders for any type of bullying behavior, even though pathological commanders are the prime culprits in workplace bullying. Sexual harassment and discrimination are actions for which a commander can face a court martial or involuntary discharge, but bullying as discussed in this book is not legally actionable.

Once a military member has been repeatedly bullying and expelled from the service, the picture may someday change. Federal magistrates, the Joint Chiefs of Staff, Surgeons General, and the Supreme Court are receiving vital information about bullying in the military workplace. In the appendix, readers can find a sample letter to a congressman or senator requesting that bullying commanders be held fully accountable to the victim, their service branch, and to their own commander.

"It is better to die on your feet than to live on your knees."
—Dolores Ibarruri

Chapter 6

Surviving Workplace Bullying & Considering Your Options

By now, the reader is armed with a vast array of comprehensive information about what constitutes workplace bullying, the kind of person who bullies, who is most likely to be selected as a bullying target, and the different types of bullying. With this information in mind, this chapter focuses on what targets and organizations can do in response to this worldwide epidemic of bad behavior. Individual options include:

Examining the target's options

- How a target can fight back against bullying and surviving the battle

- Leaving versus staying

- Repairing the damage of being targeted

- The N.I.C.E. four-point plan

- How employees can make themselves bully-proof

Organizational options include:

- Establishing a zero-tolerance policy

- Creating and implementing the "No Asshole Rule"

- Establishing and protecting professional boundaries and limits

- Prehiring psychological testing; when and how to use it

- Believing and protecting whistleblowers

Workplace bullying cannot be prevented or eliminated by one person regardless of his or her position in the organization. Nor can a small number of people accomplish this task. Creating and maintaining a zero-tolerance policy for bullying must involve the dedicated, concerted actions by every employee in the organization regardless of their job or position. Similarly, targets of bullying cannot survive or fight back alone. Since workplace bullying is an organization-wide problem, it takes the efforts of the entire organization to permanently eradicate this practice.

Once targets of workplace bullying know they have been targeted and understand what is happening to them, they must consider all their options. First, though, targets must realize that their boss, coworker, or subordinate is not just a case of "employees behaving badly." In his new, state-of-the-art book *The No Asshole Rule* (2007), Dr. Robert Sutton advises those who are disturbed and distressed about their treatment in the workplace. He recommends these methods to determine if they are being bullied:

- Talk to others; listen to other victims and bystanders who "bear the brunt of these creeps."

- Examine the Internet sites on research concerning harassment at work. Join Internet forum groups that discuss workplace bullying by those who have it or were dealing with it.

- Talk to managers, employment lawyers, consultants, and corporate coaches who struggle with "asshole management."

- Read academically researched books and eBooks on bullying, emotional abuse, petty tyranny, harassment, mobbing, and interpersonal aggression.

Should I Stay or Should I Go?

Every bullied employee has options that include staying in the workplace and slugging it out with the bully, or leaving to seek another job. Targets should be informed and thoroughly prepared before they choose between these options. Every act, positive or negative, has consequences. Targets must be ready to face the consequences of either leaving or staying.

CASE STUDY: REGINA

"I've had enough," said Regina, an employee in a retail clothing sales store. "I was so stressed from being constantly harassed on the job that I was having daily tension headaches, my moods were out of control, and I thought about suicide. Something had to change. I went to see a therapist who told me that I couldn't control the actions of others, only my own actions. I think that, for the most part, that's true. But if no one speaks up and blows the whistle on these bullies, they'll just keep on doing what they do, to me or someone else."

"I was torn between fighting back and just leaving. I knew that if I left, my boss would give me a bad reference. That would make a new job hard to find. I

CASE STUDY: REGINA

think that's one way she controlled me and kept me from talking about what she did to me. But even if I stayed, she'd continue to make my life a living hell. It seemed like I would be the loser, no matter what I did. My therapist said that no what I decided to do, I need a survival plan. I finally accepted that my working relationship with my boss wasn't repairable. I needed to deal with that and stay on the job, or else leave. I didn't want to explain to future employers why I left my last job, but at the same time I didn't want to keep on putting up with the abuse from my boss. If I stayed, I needed a suit of armor. If I left, I needed a good explanation for future employers. Either way, I was the one paying the price when I was clearly the injured party. I was dealing with something that just wasn't fair."

If You Stay

Choosing to remain in a workplace where employees are fully aware that they are targets of bullying requires many things: (1) courage, (2) a sound, dependable support system, (3) very thick skin, (4) a survival plan, and (5) a clear understanding of what they are up against.

According to Namie & Namie's research:

- 11 percent of targets transferred within the same employer

- 38 percent left voluntarily to stop further health damage

- 44 percent were terminated via employer-controlled methods

- 7 percent of bullying cases resulted in the bully being censured, transferred, or terminated

Targeted employees should be aware that these are grim statistics;

they do not account for the number of targets who remained on the job with the bully and continued to cope, making an unbearable situation bearable. Staying on the job is a thankless task; targets that choose to survive workplace bullying get no medals, plaques, or certificates of appreciation. They will never be Employee of the Month. Their friends and family members may vehemently disagree with their decision to stay. Targets may not only choose to stay and survive; they may choose also to fight back with every option they have. Confronting a bully and the upper-level managers who are indifferent, ignorant, or supportive of the bully's actions is an extremely arduous and draining task, both physically and emotionally.

Yet, others look up to the little guys who fight City Hall and win. "Americans love winners and will not tolerate losers" said General George S. Patton. Hollywood cranks out scores of movies and television shows that depict the big, bad bully laid low by the courageous "nobody" that yells, "I'm as mad as hell, and I'm not going to take this anymore!" The heroes of history are admired and held up as examples of this type of courage: the Mahatma ("Great Soul") Gandhi, a man of no particular distinction in life, quietly but decisively ended British occupation of India and helped establish "home rule" for his country. Dr. Martin Luther King would not be turned back by opposition to the Civil Rights Movement. As far back as the New Testament, the second epistle of John is addressed to the "elect lady," a pagan who converted to Christianity and was known for her charity toward others regardless of their spiritual beliefs. But before targets of bullying choose to remain on the job and resist the bully's daily barrage, they should keep in mind that sometimes the courageous journey of a thousand steps ends so, so badly: Gandhi and King were both assassinated. The elect lady and her entire family were crucified by the Romans for refusing to renounce her belief in Christ.

Martyrdom carries a heavy price. Nevertheless, those targets who muster their resources and support system and succeed in bringing down the bully have indeed accomplished a worthy goal not only for themselves, but for workers all over the globe. Fortunately, with the international spotlight turning ever more to the pervasive and insidious problem of bullying in the workplace, targets that choose to remain, survive, and fight have much more heavy artillery working for them — including the law.

> *"Let us not look back in anger, or forward in fear,*
> *But around us in awareness."*
> **—James Thurber**

Namie & Namie remark that the kiss of death for those targets who attempt to become bully-busters occurs when the bully has support all the way to the top of the organization; targets that face unanimous opposition have no chance of support. Other researchers and authors, like attorney Robert Mueller, Futterman, Davenport et al., Shapiro & Jankowski, and Sutton have different viewpoints:

Namie & Namie's position: Sacrifice your health and sanity for a paycheck? It simply does not add up. Organizations can outgun, outlast, delay, lie, and distort the truth.

Mueller's position: He who names a thing owns it. Workplace Warriors can call bullying by its name, face it down, and recapture their own power, shaking off the bully's power.

Shapiro & Jankowski's position: There is an antidote for bullies. It is possible to beat them without joining them or becoming a weak pushover.

Sutton's position: Change your mindset about what is happening to you. Avoid self-blame and develop indifference and emotional detachment toward the bully. Learn to not give a damn.

Futterman's position: Despite the risk of failure, fighting back against your bully may actually help your mental health.

Davenport et al.'s position: Disclose, blow the whistle. This is courageous and may be important for your sake and others'.

To be fair and accurate, Namie & Namie acknowledge that only the target can decide whether to stay, cope, and fight, or let Elvis leave the building forever. In addition, all the researchers and authors cited above declare that while fighting back is often worthwhile, it is just as true that targets should not feel shameful if they are unable to fight back — emotionally, physically, financially, or spiritually. In bullying cases, the issue is not how targets play the game; it is a matter of personally winning or losing. Slaying a dragon is not worth much if one is consumed and destroyed by its last dying breath of fire.

"Faith is taking that first step without being able to see the second step."
— Anonymous

There is no quarrel about faith being an admirable virtue. The Bible tells us to "walk by faith, and not by sight." Excellent advice when it comes to spirituality. Conversely, faith alone will not help targets that choose to stay, survive, and/or fight back. Staying requires a definite, well-thought-out plan to survive and cope with the bully and perhaps with the indifference of upper-level management. Targets that choose to stand their ground and fight back must develop a strategy that involves all the help they can muster. There is an old proverb that says, "If you pray for potatoes, you'd also better pick up a hoe."

Before targets develop their survival plans when they choose to stay on the job, they must make sure that their motives for staying are both rational and in their best interests. Staying just to be stubborn and unyielding is not a plan, it is a distortion in thinking that is doomed to fail. Staying to prove to the bully that targets are not incompetent, mentally unstable idiots will also fail. It is the bully's nature to form a distorted belief about the target's worth and ability and then cling to that belief regardless of all evidence to the contrary. Further, bullies come too close for comfort to the DSM-IV-TR's diagnostic criteria for the Delusional Disorder, Unspecified Type. A workplace bully hopefully has no bizarre, psychotic thoughts or beliefs about the target, but the likelihood that the target will successfully persuade the bully that he is mistaken about the target's worth is very slim. Not impossible, but not likely.

CASE STUDY: MARYBETH

"This is a true story," said MaryBeth. "It caught me by total surprise and at first I thought my leg was being pulled. But since former coworkers told me the same story, I have to believe it."

"I had a supervisor that must have come straight from Satan's Cesspool. Brad didn't like women in general and me in particular because I stood up to him. I even filed a grievance against him and won. He never forgave me for that. Then he made me miserable in every way you can think of. Constant criticism, nagging, making fun of me in front of others, giving me letters of counseling for stupid stuff, and demoting me from my position into a lesser position, he said, for the good of the company. Yeah, for his own good.

"Then one day my dream came true. He was being transferred to another location. I went to church and lit a candle! I was just glad to have outlasted him because I almost quit several times. Why should I? Let him be the one to leave, not me. And he did! I certainly didn't go to his farewell party and we left hating each other's guts."

CASE STUDY: MARYBETH

"Well, my life went on as usual, but with no conflict, dread of coming to work, crying spells, and tension headaches. Heaven on Earth. In fact, I was promoted and also reassigned to a different location. This was great because I could start fresh without his ghost walking the hallway. Then a year later, two of my former coworkers at my old location who barely know each other sent me e-mails saying that Brad had returned to the area to visit his family. He apparently asked both my old colleagues if they knew where I was and how he could get in touch with me. Brad told them both that in the past year, he had come to the realization that he had treated me badly and that he had developed a new appreciation for me. My jaw just dropped. Brad was the very last person I would have thought could change his mind about me. What could have caused this sudden epiphany?

"To this day, I don't know. My former coworkers told him where I was, and I wondered if he would contact me. I decided that I had it in my heart to be forgiving if Brad was for real. After a couple of days, I e-mailed a friend of Brad's at his new location. His friend said that Brad had only two more days on the job; he didn't say if Brad was retiring or if perhaps he was fired. After that I went on vacation for two weeks with my family, and I never did hear from Brad. So I guess I'll never know what he had to say to me. Brad was always a very haughty, arrogant guy, and for him to say what he did about treating me badly is just incredible. When he left, we certainly weren't on good terms, so something must have happened in his life that caused this change in him. It wasn't anything I did or said, that's for sure."

> *"God, grant me the serenity to accept*
> *the things I cannot change,*
> *the courage to change the things I can,*
> *and the wisdom to know the difference."*
> **— St. Francis of Assisi**

Staying Strategies

When you develop your survival plan for staying in the workplace, you should also have a backup exit plan. Putting all of your eggs in the coping baskets is a bad idea; no matter how solid your survival plan may be, there is always the chance that, as you remain in the workplace, the bullying will continue or even escalate. Keep in mind that the bully's objective is to remove you from the workplace; if you make this difficult, he or she may intensify efforts toward your destruction. It is likely to get worse before it gets better — if it ever does get better. Plan for the best, and also plan for the worst. To parody Forrest Gump, coping with and surviving workplace bullying is like a box of chocolates; you never know what result you are going to get.

Employment attorney Robert Mueller recommends several crucial parts of a target's survival plan:

- Take control over events, even if you are the only one who knows you are in control. Shake off the bully's power over you.

- View yourself as a Workplace Warrior, not a victim; victimization can cause emotional paralysis.

- Give ownership of the bully's behavior to him, not to you.

- Document in writing every incident of bullying. Jot down a few key words to describe the incident and compare those words to past incidents. Note any patterns that you observe. Include the date of the incident, time, place, person or people involved, names of witnesses, and some direct quotes of what was said to you. Include examples of how the bully's behavior negatively impacts the company's mission. If you file a grievance or civil lawsuit against the bully or the company who tolerates him, you will need this documentation to prove your case.

- Document every incident where the bully deviates from standard rules, procedures, and protocols of the workplace.

- Speak about the incident with a colleague you trust to keep your story confidential. Tell him or her everything that happened. Thoroughly document this conversation and ask if your colleague will also write a witness statement and testify in a lawsuit or grievance hearing.

- In your documentation of bullying incidents, be sure to include how the incidents made you feel physically and emotionally. In a civil suit, damages are calculated according to how much harm was done to you and the degree of harm.

- Make a decision about whether or not you plan to inform the bully that his actions are being documented by you and other witnesses. This could back the bully off considerably. It can also backfire against you if the bully resorts to more subtle, easily justifiable forms of bullying.

- Make a similar decision about informing the top-level manager that you are documenting each episode of bullying. This may capture her attention; an indifferent, lazy, or culpable manager may decide it is in his company's best interest to end the bullying.

- Make a list of the bully's "hot button" issues — those situations that seem to spark incidents of bullying. For example, the target's life after work, the target speaking to upper management about being treated unfairly, impossible tasks and deadlines that are not met, errors, no matter how minor, in a target's work performance, disliking the target's clothes and personal appearance, and a target's request for sick leave or vacation.

- Be consistent and professional in your documentation, omitting anything that could be construed as you being unstable, irrational, or vindictive. Your credibility depends on what you write and how you write it.

- After seeing a physician for a stress-related condition, a target should thoroughly document symptoms and diagnoses. The physician's actual records can be subpoenaed in a civil lawsuit along with the physician himself.

- Targets should make a well-thought-out, honest list of their strong points at work and shortcomings. This will avoid the target projecting the "halo effect" and the appearance that he or she is the perfect employee that works for a vicious, pathological bully.

"What counts is not necessarily the size of the dog in the fight, but the size of the fight in the dog."
—Dwight D. Eisenhower

The N.I.C.E. System of Beating Bullying

In their book *Bullies, Tyrants, and Impossible People* (2005), Shapiro and Jankowski recommend an entirely innovative approach to staying on the job with a workplace bully. Although not specifically mentioned, their system appears to also be applicable with those who are targets of mob bullying. These researchers and authors are both civil rights attorneys.

The N.I.C.E. system assists employees in coping with difficult people without becoming one of them. When a target is relentlessly and viciously bullied, it is too easy for him or her to retaliate in kind. Heeding the proverb that says "An eye for an eye makes the whole world blind" is a salient point for targets to keep in mind; they will accomplish nothing if they return meanness for meanness. The N.I.C.E. system consists of methods targets can put into action that are helpful for bully-busters, while they still maintain their civility and composure. Shapiro and Jankowski make it clear that using N.I.C.E. principles does not mean that targets should become passive; the system must be used by assertive targets, not "wimps."

Shapiro & Jankowski describe the N.I.C.E. system as an approach that uses a practical set of tactics that have, according to their research, been tested and proven to be effective in real-life workplaces. They believe that the N.I.C.E. system works for the following reasons:

- It enables targets to know how to respond to bullies before a difficult encounter rather than reacting on impulse.

- It assists targets in using new, effective, and nondefensive habits when dealing with a bullying situation.

- It helps targets understand what they did correctly or ineffectively so they may learn from successes and failures without repeating unhelpful mistakes in responding to bullies.

"When I am upset, I count to ten.
When I am very upset, I count to one hundred."
— Thomas Jefferson

The first and most crucial step in the N.I.C.E. system is for targets to neutralize their negative emotions toward bullies. If targets fail to rule their emotions, they will rule them. This step is not intended to suggest that targets should not acknowledge that they feel angry, frustrated, bitter, nor hateful toward the bully; it means that targets should maintain their composure during a difficult encounter with bullies. If targets respond to the bully's histrionic and intimidating behavior with calm composure, the bully loses that round. On the other hand, if targets respond with aggressive, out-of-control behavior, bullies will use this response as another weapon in their plan to destroy and oust targets from the workplace. "Disgruntled employee." "Unstable." "An anger management problem." "Insubordinate and disrespectful." These are all phrases that bullies enjoy entering into targets' personnel files as proof that the targets need to be terminated. The last thing targets should do is provide the bullies with more ammunition to make the case against them.

Each letter in the N.I.C.E. system has a corresponding meaning and strategy to survive a bullying boss:

- N = Neutralize your emotions. The more emotional you are, the less rational you will behave. The more your emotions are neutralized, the more you can be in control of a positive outcome of a bullying encounter.

- I = Identify your bully's type: (1) those people who make situations or circumstances difficult, (2) those people who believe that being unreasonable is effective, and (3) those people who have embedded personality characteristics or disorders that result in bullying behavior.

- C = Control the encounter. Once you know your enemy's

type, you can use effective techniques to determine the outcome of the encounter.

- E = Explore options. Even after you shape the outcome, you may still be at an impasse with the bully. Examine alternatives that will not make the bully feel like she has lost power over you. One important option is ending the encounter without escalating the conflict. "If you give me this stupid letter of reprimand I'm calling my lawyer" is not a good way to de-escalate the situation. Save ultimatums for instances when the best deal is no deal at all.

CASE STUDY: TERRY

Terry is a junior associate in a corporate law firm, supervised by one of the senior partners, Pam, whom he describes as "a controlling bitch." Terry often accompanied his boss to court, sitting second-chair in trial proceedings.

"She flexed her power muscles to prove that she was superior to me. I had to learn to have a very thick skin and learn to fly under the radar as much as possible. I realize that I am merely an associate and she is a senior partner but this doesn't give her the right to harass and humiliate me every moment.

"The day before we were scheduled to begin jury selection in a sizeable case, Pam called me into her office and told me that she was tired of my slovenly appearance and that we needed to present a completely professional appearance. I had no idea what she meant. I wore the best quality suits that I could afford with polished shoes and well-ironed shirts. I even ironed my ties. Pam told me that my hair was too long and insisted that I go get a haircut and then come back and show myself to her. I complied with her instructions. She wasn't satisfied with my hair and twice made me have my hair recut until I might as well have been bald.

"I was young, impressionable, and helpless. I felt singled out for Pam's daily

CASE STUDY: TERRY

criticism of my work, my demeanor, and my appearance. There was no reasoning with her. I think she believed that the way to supervise junior associates was to berate them continuously.

"The third time I appeared in her office to show her my haircut, like a ten-year-old rather than the Yale graduate that I was, she said, 'Now your hair's too short. You look like a Marine.' Finally losing my temper, I replied, 'I'd rather be a Marine in boot camp that be here putting up with your shit every day.' Not a smart thing to say, I know. She told me that she didn't take back talk from kids, and if I didn't like her shit, I should pack my stuff and get out. The situation was rapidly becoming out of control, so I apologized and backed down. I felt like a pushover. I had no one in my corner, but she had the power of all the senior partners behind her. From then on I tried to stay low and out of trouble until I could find a new job."

Terry may have been an honor graduate from Yale Law School, but in coping with his bullying boss, he gets an "F" for not following the N.I.C.E. system and escalating a situation that he was doomed to lose. Terry failed to neutralize his emotions, he did not truly understand Pam's bullying type, he had no control over the encounter, and he did not explore nonescalating options. Using N.I.C.E. principles, Terry could have done and said the following:

Terry: Okay Pam, I understand that we need to make a good impression in court. It did not occur to me that perhaps my hair was too long. Is it okay if I run out now and get a haircut? Or maybe you have a particular barber you could refer me to.

After his first haircut: Excuse me, Pam, but I went to the barber you suggested and I think he did a fine job. I need for you to specifically tell me what part of my hair is still too long so that I can tell the barber.

After his second haircut: Pam, there is nothing wrong with my hair. I did and said exactly as you instructed. Perhaps you can accompany me back to the barber to be certain he cuts my hair according to your specifications. Then hopefully we can move on and discuss our questions for the jury pool.

After his third haircut: Pam, you said you were too busy to go with me to the barber. I have now paid for three haircuts, and I cannot really afford this. I cannot instantly regrow hair that you now think is too short. I have no more hair left to cut, so I would appreciate it if we could move on to important matters. By the way, my brother is a real spit-and-polish Marine and I consider it a compliment if I look like him.

"It is time you left....100,000 Englishmen simply cannot control 350,000,000 Indians if those Indians refuse to cooperate. That is what we intend to achieve – peaceful, non-violent non-cooperation until you see the wisdom of leaving, Your Excellency."
—Mohandas K. Gandhi
Speaking to Lord Irwin, Viceroy of India regarding independence from England

The Mahatma Gandhi is a prime example of putting the N.I.C.E. principles into effective action. Gandhi was a pacifist who never uttered an angry threat of violence toward the British occupation forces in India. When violence did erupt in India regarding home rule, Gandhi went on a nearly fatal hunger strike until all Indians put down their weapons. Gandhi's most powerful quality was his calm, respectful, and assertive manner in speaking with the English Viceroy and other officers about India's home rule. For Gandhi, violence, force, and rage were not options. He was always in control of his emotions. He knew his adversaries so well as people whose situation and circumstances made them bullies. Gandhi was always in control of every encounter with British officers because he was in control of himself. Rather than escalate the already fiery relations between Indians and the British occupying army, Gandhi merely explained what he hoped that India would and would not do to achieve home rule without uttering an inflammatory word that could have rapidly escalated the circumstances into all-out bloodshed. Instead of giving ultimatums, Gandhi expressed his belief that the British themselves would decide to leave India, and that is just what happened.

Sutton's Tips for Surviving in a "Pro-Asshole" Organization

In his book *The No Asshole Rule*, Dr. Robert Sutton notes that millions of workers are trapped in organizations where the "pro-asshole" conditions apply, normally for financial reasons. If this is a situation that affects a lot of bullying targets, Sutton supplies some survival tips that could help make targets' lives at least bearable:

- Avoid self-blame for having become a target. Bullying is all about the bully, not the target. Targets should never link their sense of self-worth with how the bully treats them.

- Maintain emotional detachment from the bully's abusive tirades; again, it is not about the target, it is about the bully. Disregard anything that insults your soul.

- Develop "learned optimism" and view being bullied as a temporary situation. Sooner or later, either the target or the bully will move on, up, or out.

- While hoping for the best, targets should expect the worst. This can be achieved if targets lower their expectations of the bully and the workplace in general.

- Look for small victories rather than large-scale changes. If targets maintain the power to control small aspects of their workplace circumstances, this can have a big impact upon their well-being as well as reducing their sense of hopelessness and helplessness.

- Targets can use a variety of measures to limit their exposure to bullies. Communicating via written memos and e-mails prevents, at least to some degree, going face-to-face with demeaning, humiliating bullies' tirades. Targets can also remain standing rather than being seated when called into the bully's office to make a quick exit if necessary. This approach also has the benefit of subliminally suggesting to the bully that their target really is not interested in what he or she has to say.

- Find and build some vital pockets of support at work among kind, decent people. Targets need to discover that the entire organization is not filled with insensitive jerks.

"Don't tell me I'm wrong, don't tell me that you knew all along
I won't roll over dead; only I know what goes on in my head
I've got nothing to hide; I'm not guilty inside
I'm not going away!
You try so hard to break me,
But all your diamonds turn to sand."
"I'm Not Going Away"
By O. Osbourne, Z. Wylde, and K. Churko

Targets that choose to stand their ground and fight must

develop a firm resolve that they are not going away, not giving up or giving in. Since the path to bully-busting is all uphill, this resolve is often the only thing that keeps targets in the workplace gladiatorial arena. Namie & Namie describe three crucial bully-busting approaches:

1) Targets can trust and use internal grievance procedures against bullies. However, these policies were not written for employees' rights, but to shield the organization. Expect hurdles, delays, and double standards, and continuing attacks by the bully.

2) Targets can hire a bully to fight their case with them.

3) Targets can mount an internal, informal campaign to go outside normal channels while seeking justice against the bullies and the organization that tolerates them.

One of the purposes of bully-busting is to provide targets with the opportunity and the means to regain their dignity and self-respect. Targets who stay on the job can accomplish this by developing a solid support system of friends, coworkers, family members, a physician, and a therapist. To succeed and survive, targets need some nonjudgmental "listening ears" who can assure them that they are not fighting alone. It is important that targets' support systems not tell them what to do and how to do it, but that they support and empathize with the targets. Those targets that need advice about what to do will ask for it. While bullies are more often than not in positions of power and authority, targets' support systems meet them on an equal level and have no personal agenda.

Workplace bullies are like cockroaches; shine the light on them and they run for cover. Some targets choose to make their stories public through the media, becoming blatant whistleblowers. Newspaper and magazine articles pack a powerful punch; some targets consider hiring a professional writer to help them tell their stories. Targets can also consult their unions to request mediation through the union's legal department.

Namie & Namie's Workplace Bullying Institute, found on the Internet as **www.bullyinginstitute.org**, developed a whistleblower's checklist, authored by Tom Devine, Legal Director of the Government Accountability Project. They stress that when "crying foul" in the workplace, whistleblowing targets of bullying face the prospect of losing their jobs; by silencing the messenger, the organization can cover up serious warning signals of subsequent disasters like the targets' suicide and workplace violence. Others who are bullied, then, are less likely to come forward and speak about what is happening within the organization. Devine's checklist for whistleblowers includes:

- Make memorandums for a record of every bullying incident. (Earlier sections of this chapter discussed how to accomplish this.)

- Identify and copy all necessary supporting documents like organizational policies, work performance records, and medical/mental health records. If this is not possible, make a list of records that exist but are unobtainable, and where they are located for the benefit of investigators or courts.

- Create a larger support circle that consists of others who will benefit from blowing the whistle on bullying.

- Seek help from specialists, e.g., employment attorneys, civil rights attorneys, mental health experts, physicians, and others who can play key roles in busting the bullies.

- Learn how to navigate the legal landscape via an attorney who is familiar with whistleblowing. Once an organization is challenged and exposed, upper-level managers may fire back with legal counterattacks, threats, and even filing lawsuits against the whistleblower. Targets should make sure they understand the legal definitions and required proof of libel, slander, defamation, wrongful termination, actual damages, and punitive damages. Targets should also supply their attorney with potential witnesses to bolster their case.

- Whistleblowers must develop survival strategies to cope with the almost certain prospect of having all their own faults, errors, and dirty laundry exposed to discredit them. Expect that the bully or organization will make every attempt to destroy the whistleblower's credibility.

- Examine the motivation for whistleblowing; targets who merely seek revenge against a bully or organization should rethink their plan. The same can be said for targets who seek only their fifteen minutes of fame and attention. Today's news lines tomorrow's birdcage. The public has a short attention span, but whistleblowers must live their lives carrying the memories of the long, difficult fight for justice and change.

- Consider trying to work within the system before going public. Targets should first exhaust all internal relief systems, if any, before breaking ranks. Failed attempts to work within the organization's grievance system should be carefully and completely documented; not doing this reflects poorly on a whistleblower's credibility.

- Whistleblowers should consult their families before going public. Although targets face enormous hardships at work because of bullying, challenging the system can cause considerable family problems. Supportive families can also provide targets with a soft place to fall during this gut-wrenching period because a person who is loved and appreciated at home cannot be completely degraded by bullies.

- Keep a detailed record of all events before and after the whistle is sounded. Document any seemingly retaliation-oriented acts by the bully and the organization. Targets should not include speculation, personal opinions, or animosity toward the bully and the organization.

"When injuries result from the worksite exposure to chemical substances, the offending institutions are compelled to introduce remedies. When the injuries originate from toxic human behavior, no less should occur."
—Harvey Hornstein
Brutal Bosses and Their Prey

Surviving Mob Bullying

Targets who have been mob bullied have unique issues besides those encountered by one bullying boss. Staying on the job and coping with mobbers means single-handedly engaging in combat with an army, not just the general. Being mob bullied leaves awfully deep emotional scars; sometimes the target feels as if she will never truly find peace and serenity. For many targets, the effects of what they endured last a lifetime; they are forever changed in the way they see themselves and others. As an example, we can revisit the case of Siobhan, who was mob bullied.

CASE STUDY: SIOBHAN

"I did try to fight back," said Siobhan, "but I was so outnumbered and overpowered that I knew I didn't stand a chance. A friend told me that the secretary of the top manager was overheard talking about my case in a derogatory manner in a local bank. My humiliation was spread around for the public's amusement. I was totally stripped of my dignity and my good name. These things will never return to me, not ever."

"Before I exercised my right to a termination hearing, I went through every grievance procedure in the organization and not one thing was done to help me. Now that I understand that I was mob bullied, I realize that I was just one 'small fish' and had no one to count on except my family. Without my knowledge or permission, my husband called the top manager and told him, 'You're killing my wife.' Apparently, the top boss didn't care if he killed me because nothing changed.

"I tried to maintain some humor about my situation; I referred to my workplace as 'Azkaban,' the wizard's prison in the Harry Potter books. I signed e-mails to friends 'From the Prisoner of Azkaban.' But after almost two years of being mobbed, all my strength was gone, and I still had to go through the termination hearing. Listening to them lie and misstate the truth was like being mobbed all over again, just as I was when I followed the grievance procedures. During that time, I was mobbed over and over again, even by people who were supposed to help me find relief and people who took oaths to tell the truth and then committed perjury.

"My appointed attorney told me that when he discussed my case with the top boss, he said, 'We're just going to get rid of her.' Without even knowing me, he already decided what was going to happen to me. He became one of the mob. What made me laugh out loud is that the organization was promoting a new program to reduce workplace stress and suicide prevention."

CASE STUDY: SIOBHAN

"What the mob did to me was the exact opposite of the top boss's own program. It applied to everyone but me because not one person gave a damn about me.

"After losing the termination hearing, my appointed attorney filed an appeal to the organization's head office. I didn't wait around to see the outcome; I just got the hell out of there because if I didn't, I knew something very, very bad was going to happen to me or to them. I guess you could say that I was fired and I quit on the same day. The final irony is that three months after I left, I received a letter from the top boss at the head office; it said that my local top boss should not have instituted termination proceedings against me and that all his actions did not follow the organization's established procedure. Also, the state where I worked sent me a letter saying that my certification in my job specialty had been restored and my local top boss's complaint to my certification board had been dismissed. I wasn't really happy about being vindicated; it just made me angrier at the mob. Too little, too late. My life was ruined and I will never be the same."

To cope with mob bullying on the job, Davenport et al. recommend the following strategies:

- Go through a grieving process about emotional, physical, and occupational losses.

- Believe in the value of change.

- Seek the support of family and friends.

- Have a pet — the only unconditional love that money can buy.

- Do not isolate yourself.

- Gain strength from the things you love.

- Be with positive people and do things to rebuild your self-esteem.

- Use your existing skills in another context.

- Learn a new skill.

- Stop "victim" thoughts.

- Understand that you are in control of yourself and you do have choices.

- Distance yourself from the workplace when you can.

- It is only a job; it is what you do, not who you are.

- Keep a journal of positive self-affirmations.

- Recognize and use the power of humor.

- See a therapist and make the organization pay the bill.

Making a Graceful and Practical Exit

"Take This Job and Shove It!" was a popular song three decades ago, and it still expresses the thoughts and feelings of the targets that choose to leave a bullying workplace with style. No exit drama, tearful recriminations to bullies, nor undignified scenes. Just drop off the key, Lee, and get yourself free. Robert Mueller suggests that targets that choose to leave should do so with happiness and excitement about the future, not agony about the past. Up to the moment when targets walk out the door for the last time, targets who display a "winning" victorious attitude as they leave annoy bullies to no end; it takes away their credit for supposedly conquering and disposing of their targets. Workplace

Warriors must separate themselves from "ground zero" physically, emotionally, and spiritually; organizations are large burdens for targets to carry around on their backs for the rest of their lives, as exemplified by Siobhan's story. Instead of obsessing about what happened to them in the workplace, former targets must understand that they think about the bullies much more than the bullies think about them. With a winning, victorious attitude, former targets can make their exit a day of joy rather than a day of hate and misery. When they drive away from their former workplace on that last day with a smile, targets have taken the first step in regaining their lives, dignity, self-worth, and personal power. Their parting thought directed toward the bully and the workplace should be, "Get out of my way!"

> *"Though we cannot bring back that hour of splendor in the grass and glory in the flowers, we will grieve not —*
> *but find strength in what remains behind."*
> **— Walt Whitman**

In addition to the grace with which former targets leave an accursed, toxic workplace, there are several practical matters to consider. Susan Futterman and this author suggest the following "exit" checklist:

1) Consider your financial situation and try to time your exit accordingly. Check your bank accounts, your spouse or partner's ability to "carry you" until you find another job, and make sure all your insurance payments are current. Check the balances on your credit cards; satisfy yourself that you can at least make the minimum payment until you are employed again and avoid using credit cards.

2) Create a list of necessary expenditures and possible sources

of temporary income; plan for unexpected financial issues. Include any stocks, bonds, IRAs, 401(k) plans, annuities, pensions, stock options, rent or mortgage payments, alimony, and child support payments either due or received. Prioritize your expenses and list what can wait or be eliminated.

3) Try not to leave abruptly without an exit plan, but if you have to go, then go.

4) Muster all your marketable skills. You may not even want a job similar to your former job. Maybe it is time to try something different and in which you are competent.

5) Prior to your departure, polish your resume and reference letters. Many job seekers hire a professional writer to assist them with these tasks.

6) Determine your eligibility for social security benefits, Veteran's benefits, unemployment payments, and workers' compensation benefits.

7) Once you have decided to leave the job, give notice to your employer, even if he or she is the bully. Through mediation, you may be able to negotiate a severance package such as a monetary settlement and continued medical benefits for 60-90 days. This may be an appropriate time for you to calmly but firmly make a few veiled threats about whistleblowing. Your employer may decide that it is better to pay you off than to prolong the battle. The bully is getting what he wants — you are leaving. If he has an ounce of common sense, you will be allowed to leave the easy way rather than the hard way that will benefit no one.

8) When negotiating your exit, if your employer asks you to sign a nondisclosure agreement which contains an agreement not to file a lawsuit against him or her, strongly consider this option. In return, ask the boss to sign a "generic" letter of reference (that you wrote yourself, detailing your strengths) instead of giving you a nasty reference to future employers. Apply the *quid pro quo* strategy; both of you benefit and get what you want.

9) Consult a credit counselor to consolidate your debts at a reduced payment or reduced interest rate.

10) To be competitive in today's job market, you may need to obtain credit hours in your desired field through a college or technical school. Ask about scholarships, grants, and student loans.

11) Use up all your sick days and vacation time; go job hunting while you are away from the workplace prior to your permanent departure. Never talk with a potential employer about what you suffered in your soon-to-be former workplace; this could be a mark of "trouble." No one wants to hire a problem child.

"The people who get on in this world are people who get up and look for the circumstances they want, and, if they can't find them, they make them."
—George Bernard Shaw

Organizational Options

In addition to targets of bullying having viable options when deciding to stay or leave an organization, organizations themselves have options: (1) establishing a zero-tolerance policy by creating Sutton's "No Asshole Rule," (2) remaining indifferent and uninformed about the existence of workplace bullying, and (3) direct or indirect complicity with bullying behaviors. The first option is difficult but worthwhile and critical to accomplishing the mission of the organization. The second and third options are nonproductive, dangerous, inhumane, and open doors for legal action by the targets of bullying.

> *"We teach people how to treat us."*
> **— Dr. P. C. McGraw**

Television's beloved "Dr. Phil" not only hosts America's most popular talk show, he is also a well-respected clinical psychologist in his own right. In his book *Life Strategies*, Dr. McGraw explains that if people want to be treated with respect and dignity, they must indicate to everyone in their lives that they will accept nothing less; we must take ownership of our behaviors that tell others how they must treat us. If we are treated badly, we need to take stock of our behaviors that reinforce, elicit, or allow such treatment. For example, victims of domestic violence who remain in a destructive relationship in which they are subjected to more abuse teach their abuser that he or she can continue that behavior without fear of the consequences of their actions. Choosing the actions means choosing the consequences.

Applying Dr. McGraw's principle to workplace bullying means that targets who allow bullying teach the bully that they will tolerate ill-treatment without complaint. In organizations that turn a blind eye to bullying by either indifference or complicity, passive targets teach these organizations that they need not be proactive by enacting and enforcing zero-tolerance policies. While being bullied is never the target's fault, every target should ask herself the crucial question, "What am I doing or not doing that is teaching them that they can treat me like this? I'm mad as hell, and I'm not going to take this anymore!" This is the all-important first step toward bringing about organizational change regarding workplace bullying. Life rewards action, not passivity.

Bullies, like serial killers, don't just stop; they are stopped by organizational policies that, if not followed, would result in their termination. In *The No Asshole Rule*, Sutton discusses reasons why organizations need the rule: mean-spirited bullies cause massive damage to their targets, bystanders who receive the "ripple" effect, the organization's performance, and themselves. When deciding whether establishing and enforcing a no asshole rule is needed in an organization, top-level managers should "do the math" about how the organization is affected by asshole bullies in the workplace, a step called the Total Cost of Assholes (TCA). An accounting must be made in terms of the costs of human relations problems that diminish employees' motivation and work performance, physical stress-related illnesses and missed work, opening the organization up to legal action, time spent "cooling off" both bullies and targets, time spent interviewing new personnel if either the bully or the target departs from the organization, the cost of rehabilitation programs like anger and stress management, and letting competitors gain the advantage over an asshole-afflicted organization. It just is not efficient for organizations to tolerate assholes.

Implementing a no asshole rule, according to Sutton, involves several steps:

- Clearly define the prohibited behavior; spell out specifically what behavior constitutes being an asshole, including bullying.

- Make it public. Every employee should have written notice of the rule, and also conduct mandatory briefings about the rule. Make it clear that assholes cannot hide from the impact of the rule.

- Require every employee to read and sign the rule, eliminating the "I didn't know" excuse.

- When new employees are hired and oriented to the workplace, make sure they know and understand the rule and the consequences of breaking it.

- Weave the rule into hiring and firing policies. Before hiring new staff members, introduce them to the people that they will be working for, working with, or supervising. Seek feedback from these employees before signing on a new staff member; others often have negative or positive vibes about this stranger who may be in their midst.

- Apply the rule to customers and clients. It is not good business to allow employees to be bullied and abused by anyone.

- Beware of differences in status or power among employees. Assholes in charge are dangerous; they are aware of their power and they know how to abuse it by bullying. Leaders get paid more because they have the ability to make their workplace profitable. This will not happen with leaders who "lead" by bullying and being assholes.

- Focus on conversations and interactions. Pay attention to what is said and done in every work station. Do not disregard grievances and complaints filed by targets; even if the target is being a bit histrionic, there is always a grain of truth in every complaint.

- Teach people how to fight assholes. Encourage them to use internal grievance procedures if they feel that they are being mistreated. Make them aware that they do have options and remedies that will be taken seriously by upper-level management.

- Be slow to "brand" people. Too many targets are dismissed as "disgruntled employees" to protect the organization's integrity. Yet, it is a distinct violation of an asshole's bullying target to be branded as mentally unstable or seeking a civil court settlement. Upper-level managers must hear and determine for themselves the target's credibility instead of automatically adopting the bully's point of view of the target.

> *"Joe Gold, who established the famous Gold's Gyms,*
> *applied the rule to his gyms, just as he did in his home.*
> *No jerks allowed. One of his customers was Arnold*
> *Schwarzenegger, who won seven Mr. Olympia titles."*
> **Dr. Robert Sutton**
> *The No Asshole Rule*

Once a no asshole rule has been implemented in a workplace to prevent bullying, it is useless unless it is enforced. Just having the rule is not sufficient. Organizations focus on "big" things like making profits through better, faster, and cheaper procedures, and on "small" things like how people within the workplace actually treat one another. Sutton provides ten steps to enforcing the no asshole rule:

- Say the rule, write it down, and act on it. Making false claims and promises to bullied employees is worse than having no asshole-prevention policy at all.

- Prevent assholes from hiring other assholes. Keep them out of the hiring process; they tend to hire people like themselves.

- Get rid of assholes fast. Organizations often wait too long to relieve themselves of assholes who are interfering with the company's mission.

- Treat assholes as incompetent. Though they may do some things well, if they persist in demeaning and bullying others, they are incompetent.

- Remember that power breeds nastiness. Sometimes giving power to seemingly benign employees quickly turns them into assholes.

- Embrace the power-performance paradox. Organizations have pecking orders; this does not mean that those with power can abuse those without.

- Manage moments, not just practices, policies, and systems. Upper-level managers who focus on the "small" things like human interactions will then find that big changes occur.

- Teach and model constructive confrontation. There is a time and a place for arguing; individuals can disagree without becoming disagreeable. All confrontations should be respectful of the dignity of both parties.

- Adopt the "one asshole rule." Employees follow rules and norms better if they have a visible example of what constitutes being an asshole. As long as they do not do any real damage, employees learn the rights and wrongs of interactions.

- Link big policies to small decencies. A workplace-wide no asshole rule works best when the rule effects how people talk and work together.

Living a no asshole way of life establishes the manner in which employees work together and how they work with customers. The mission of entire organizations can be scuttled by just a few demeaning creeps. Sutton notes that negative interactions have five times the effect on our moods than positive interactions. Thus, it takes a lot of kind, supportive, decent people to make up for the damage caused by one asshole. People tend to remember and internalize negative reflections on their competency and character more than they do positive feedback interactions. It is the little moments that matter most to a bullying target. A supportive smile from a coworker, a compliment from the top boss, and not treating workers as if they were invisible automatons go a long way in helping a target deflect and heal hurts caused by bullying assholes. When an organization implements and enforces the no asshole rule, those who abide by it are rewarded with respect and appreciation; rule violators should be confronted with painful, and sometimes public, embarrassment. Organizations that want to increase their productivity via motivated, content workers need to push the "delete" key on bullying assholes.

It has not been so long ago that victims of domestic violence, rape, child abuse, and elder abuse were not believed when they described what happened to them. Physical and sexual abusers are so adept in their bullying behavior and so convincing in their stories of "who, me?" that they sounded very credible to investigators. This has changed considerably. Law enforcement and mental health professionals have learned to listen to and believe victims of maltreatment. The same change has occurred in many workplaces; bullying is merely another form of abuse. Many employee assistance programs, mediation programs, therapists, lawyers, and clergy members are trained in assisting targets of workplace bullying. If these helpers understand the dynamics of the workplace, bullying bosses and coworkers will have a better ability to help targets cope with bullying and, if they choose, to become whistleblowers. As a substitute of feeling isolated and invisible, targets grow to feel that others understand and believe them. This is normally true in all organizations except the armed forces where bullying by superiors and mob bullying is rampant and protected. This will not change until some drastic policy changes regarding bullying in the military are set and strictly enforced by the Surgeons General and Chiefs of Staff at the Pentagon.

Davenport et al. suggest a number of warning signs that bullying exists within an organization with an emphasis on mob bullying:

- Significant changes without preparing employees. Unexpected changes by bullies cause fear and uncertainty. Since bullies feel that they need not discuss changes with anyone lower on the workplace pecking order, they do what they want, when they want to do it.

- One individual has suddenly become a target. All organizations have a "grapevine" or "rumor mill." When word gets to top-level managers that an employee has become an undeserving target of assaults upon his or her personal or professional reputation, this should prick up the ears of top-level managers and give them cause to wonder if bullying or mob bullying is occurring in a work station.

- Alliances across the hierarchy of an organization. Company employees are always looking for a way up the hierarchy that sometimes involves playing internal political games. If this behavior goes to the length of involving subordinates who are threatened or otherwise bullied into supporting one or another individual, refusal to play the game can quickly result in mobbing by the individual's supporters. It does no good for an employee to say, "I don't have a dog in this fight;" by then, everyone is required to take sides.

- Anarchy can be an unintended result of organizational bullying; it can also be deliberately unleashed as a tactic of mobbing. The focus of the organization becomes the goal of the company rather than its intended profitable mission.

- Reduction in quality and quantity of work. Bullies in the workplace damage team motivation and cohesion. Unhappy targets and bystanders do not do their best work.

- Loss of the organization's reputation. Sooner or later, targets talk to friends and family, attorneys, therapists, even the media. A good reputation takes years to create, but only a short time to destroy.

- Increased employee turnover. If at all possible, targets and bystanders who think they may become the next target leave. Since the organization has not cared enough about them to stop the bullying, they feel no loyalty to stay with the company.

- Increased sick leave and workers' compensation claims that are the direct result of stress-related physical and emotional illnesses. These problems costs money for an organization by paying the tab out of its own pocket.

Davenport et al. provide an example of a organizational policy that is similar to Sutton's no asshole policy. This example is contained in the Appendix.

They also point out that an increasing number of organizations are focusing on behavioral risk management. While human relations consultants may not yet be familiar with all aspects of bullying, especially mob bullying, the symptoms and results of bullying cannot be ignored.

"I knew when I established standards and they were not followed by my subordinates, someone above me told them they didn't have to and not to listen to me. This same person told them to come to her if there was something I did that they didn't like."

Joan
**From *Mobbing: Emotional Abuse
in the American Workplace***

Chapter 7

Bullying & the Law

"Watch what you say — they'll be calling you a radical, a liberal fanatical, a criminal..."
"The Logical Song"
Written and performed by Supertramp

Setting the Precedents

Bullying, standing alone, is not a cause of action in American civil courts. Nonetheless, some behavior habitually stemming from bullies in the workplace are actionable. In 1998, two Supreme Court decisions made employers responsible for harassment and discrimination by employees who were acting as agents of the employer, e.g., midlevel managers and worksite supervisors. *Burlington Industries v. Ellerth* and *Faragher v. City of Boca Raton* both made history by holding senior management of organizations liable for the behavior of their abusive employees. In March 2005, the first so-called "bullying trial" resulted in a $325,000 verdict against a bullying Indianapolis surgeon. In August 2005, a jury awarded $366 million to a physician bullied by abuse of the peer review process. In February 2006, a teacher received a settlement of $500,000 in a defamation lawsuit filed against the school district.

The tide is turning, and movements to eliminate or legally punish forms of workplace bullying are gathering steam according to Carolyn Said, a seasoned news writer and journalist, in her 2007 article, "Bullying Bosses Could Be Busted: Movement Against Worst Workplace Abusers Gains Momentum With Proposed Laws." Proposed laws cannot outlaw workplace bullying, but would require employers to correct and prevent bullying and give targets the right to sue for actual and punitive damages. As might be suspected, employers oppose such legislation, referring to it as an invitation to frivolous lawsuits; it is sometimes difficult to determine if an employee is a bona fide target of workplace bullying as opposed to being a troublesome, unhappy worker. Grassroots lobbyists in California hope to gain support for antibullying legislation but fear that Governor Schwarzenegger will be reluctant to sign a bill that imposes mandates on private sector organizations.

Montana, New Jersey, and Oklahoma will consider passing antibullying legislation in 2008. New York, Kansas, Missouri, Massachusetts, Hawaii, Washington, and Oregon introduced this type of legislation in the past two years, but they were not passed. Antibullying laws do exist in Australia, England, France, Germany, Sweden, Switzerland, and the Canadian province of Quebec without resulting in a flood of sue-your-boss lawsuits that have no merit. Despite the fact that putting the brakes on bullying would in reality benefit organizations by increasing morale and productivity, plus lower health costs due to stressed-out targets of bullying, top-level managers of organizations are "hard-wired" to support midlevel managers and supervisors over the rank-and-file workers; the boss is always right.

Susan Futterman makes the point that although employees may be targets of bullying and other abuses, they may not have the basis for a successful lawsuit. Currently, employees who are mistreated in the workplace have no legal recourse that specifically addresses bullying unless the target has the "protected status" of being discriminated against due to gender, nationality, race, religion, age, or those specifics covered by the Americans With Disabilities Act of 1990, Age Discrimination in Employment Act of 1967, or the Civil Rights Act of 1964.

Despite the recent "wins" in harassment and defamation cases, bullying targets cannot look to the courts for antibullying decisions for plaintiffs; at least not yet. In 1998, Supreme Court Justice Antonin Scalia, writing the majority opinion, stated that "the law does not prohibit all verbal and physical harassment in the workplace." A District of Columbia newspaper responded to this decision in an editorial calling for Congress to write specific antiharassment laws that do not require sex, race, or national origin protections, but instead, these laws should cover a work environment that is sufficiently abusive. Namie & Namie note that in 77 percent of cases, there was legally actionable cause for discrimination because the target was not a member of a protected status group. The only class of individuals with a lower success rate in discrimination and harassment is incarcerated criminals.

Understanding the Legal Language

When speaking about causes of action against bullies and their employees, some legal definitions must be understood:

- A tort is a wrongful act that results in injury to another person's property or reputation for which the injured person is entitled to seek legal redress (Davenport et al.).

- Defamation includes the tort actions of libel and slander. Libel consists of written statements, and slander consists of spoken statements and/or misleading or deceptive photographs and videotapes. To prevail in a case of defamation, the plaintiff must (1) prove that defamatory, false statements that damaged the reputation of the plaintiff were made by the defendant, (2) prove that the defamatory statement was communicated to a person other than the plaintiff, (3) prove that the defendant knew the statement to be false or behaved in a manner that demonstrates a reckless disregard for the truth, and (4) prove that he or she was financially harmed by the defamation.

- The burden of proof in civil tort actions is by preponderance of the evidence rather than the criminal burden of beyond a reasonable doubt. This lesser burden of proof requires that the evidence presented at trial is tilted toward either the plaintiff or the defendant.

- Truth is an absolute defense in defamation cases. To prove this element, the defendant must be able to produce evidence that what he or she wrote or said about the plaintiff is true.

- Special harm is required as evidence by the plaintiff to show that he or she has suffered harm of a pecuniary (economic) nature. This means that even if the plaintiff can prove that the defendant's slander or libel caused him or her to become physically ill or emotionally distressed, this is not sufficient to constitute special harm unless the plaintiff can also prove that other people's opinions of the plaintiff was lowered.

- Damages in a case of defamation can involve both actual damages of economic loss, such as being fired or demoted, and punitive damages that punish a defendant for knowingly or recklessly defaming the plaintiff. A successful plaintiff can also request that the defendant pay all court costs and attorney fees as part of their damages.

- Intentional infliction of emotional distress is defined by the courts as "extreme and outrageous" conduct that was intended to, and did, cause harm to the plaintiff.

- Wrongful termination may apply to an employee's case if he or she was fired, laid off, forced to quit, or forced to retire. These cases usually occur as a result of discrimination involving an employee with "protected status," but of late, courts have been finding for plaintiffs who were exposed to harmful bad conduct and a hostile working environment.

- Constructive discharge occurs when the plaintiff is forced to work in a workplace that is so intolerable that any reasonable person would feel compelled to quit. Producing a paper trail of documentation of intolerable, toxic working conditions and the testimony of other targets and/or coworkers are essential in proving a plaintiff's case. Unwarranted demotion, salary cuts, reduced job responsibilities, reassignment to menial or degrading work, harassment, and humiliation are examples of situations that could be cited as constructive discharge.

- Retaliatory discharge occurs when an employee files a complaint or grievance against a manager or supervisor and he or she is fired in retaliation. To prevail, the plaintiff must prove that the employer's action was retaliatory.

- Individual liability and employer liability may or may not be connected. An employer who knows — or should have known — that an employee is being grossly mistreated by a manager or supervisor and does not intervene can be held liable for the harm suffered by the plaintiff. When a manager or supervisor acts beyond the scope of his or her duties as an agent of the employer, the employer can request severance from the plaintiff's suit and make the individual abuser face trial alone.

CASE STUDY: JANE DOE, PLAINTIFF, V. ACME ORGANIZATION AND JOHN DOE, DEFENDANTS

Jane Doe, age 48, has worked for Acme for nine years and has an excellent work record. Last year, John Doe was hired by Acme as a midlevel manager in Jane's workplace. Jane found that her personality style and John's were exceptionally different. Jane was outgoing, friendly, informal, and a bit eccentric as evidenced by her liking of heavy metal rock music and her chic but unusual hair style and clothing. Given that Jane did not work directly with customers, her differences had been well tolerated by her coworkers, all of whom liked her a great deal.

Shortly after John arrived at Acme, he called Jane into his office and told her that she couldn't listen to her music at work, even on her iPod where no one else could hear it, her hair and clothing style wouldn't be tolerated; she needed to dress and groom herself like other female employees, and that she was too cheerful in morning staff meetings when other employees were still sluggish and barely awake. John told Jane that there had been no complaints made about her from other employees, but he himself found her personality style to be annoying. Jane complied with John's instructions. John, however, continued to harass Jane about the quality of her work which, until John arrived, had been praised unequivocally by her previous manager.

It was soon evident that Jane and John did not think highly of each other. One day, a friend of Jane's told her that John was required to brief new Acme employees about maintaining professional bearing. The friend told Jane that she

CASE STUDY: JANE DOE, PLAINTIFF, V. ACME ORGANIZATION AND JOHN DOE, DEFENDANTS

overheard John saying, "If you want to see an example of piss-poor professional bearing, visit my section and say hello to Jane Doe. She's the opposite of what an Acme employee should be, and she won't make it here much longer. If you want to succeed at Acme, stay far away from Jane." After this incident, which Jane and her friend both documented, Jane found that none of the new employees would speak to her, introduce themselves, or even make eye contact with her.

While meeting with a top-level manager for his probationary period review, Jack Doe was asked about relationships with coworkers; Jack replied, "I'm okay with everyone but Jane Doe. John told us that she was trouble, and to stay away from her. Since we're new, we don't think much of her and don't want to work with her." The senior manager did not follow up on Jack's comments about Jane. Another midlevel supervisor in a different section told the Acme senior manager that during a meeting where 15 other managers were present that Jane Doe was "a piece of trash and I don't want sluts like her in my section. She'll soon be out of here; I'll make it happen." Still the senior manager did not investigate this information.

When it was time for Jane's annual performance report, she read the report and noted that John had written that she was an alcoholic, had stolen money from other women's purses, was insubordinate and rude to him, incompetent, and was mentally unstable; none of these statements were true. Jane filed an internal grievance against John for lying about her in her performance report. Two weeks later, Jane was laid off from her job and told by John to find a new job because she would be the last employee to return to Acme.

Jane hired an attorney and sued Acme Organization and John Doe for slander, libel (defamation), and wrongful termination. At trial, Jane was able to prove via documentation and witnesses that the burden of proof in her case was met. The jury found in Jane's favor against both Acme and John Doe. Jane was awarded $36,000 in actual damages for one year's loss of income and $2,000,000 in punitive damages.

It is clear that Jane was the target of a bullying boss who picked the wrong person to defame. John's slanderous and libelous statements about Jane were not only untrue, but cost Jane her professional reputation and good name. According to Emanuel's law outline on torts, insulting or profane language toward an employee are not sufficient to establish a cause of action in a civil suit for intentional infliction of emotional distress. This sort of bullying boss is best dealt with through the no asshole policy. In Jane's case, John made no defamatory statement to her, but he did communicate slanderous and libelous statements about Jane to other people, thus meeting one of the requirements of a successful case of defamation.

Jane's case also illustrates the issue of defamation via written (libelous) performance reports by a bullying boss. According to attorney David Hurd, toxic bullies can be held legally accountable for defamatory comments about a target when the defamatory statement is made under any of these circumstances:

- Without a good faith belief that the statement is true

- Without reasonable grounds for believing the truth of the statement

- With the motive or willingness to vex, harass, annoy, or injure the target

- Is exaggerated or not fully or fairly stated

- The result of a reckless investigation

- Motivated by ill will toward the target

Hurd further explains that courts have held performance reports to be defamatory if they involve allegations of embezzlement, lying, irresponsibility, lack of integrity, dishonesty, laziness, incompetence, not being eligible for rehire, insubordination, being a traitor to the company, or having committed a crime. Several of these factors were present in Jane's case.

Since truth is an absolute defense in defamation cases of libel and slander, the employer or boss has the burden of proof in bringing the affirmative defense of proving that the statement in question is true. The allegedly defamatory statement must also state a fact, not an opinion or innuendo. There is a catch here, though: a bullied target that makes a true statement to a hostile boss such as being in recovery for chemical dependence or being treated for depression has certainly behaved unwisely, but may prevail in a case of invasion of privacy when this statement was used to downgrade the target's performance report. Annual appraisals are reviewed by several "higher-ups" before they become a matter of record. The legal question is whether the target, in speaking with his or her boss, had a reasonable expectation of privacy.

A useful legal remedy in cases of serial or mob bullying is the class action lawsuit. Individual targets may share their stories with other employees who state that they have had very similar problems with the exact same people. All have attempted to resolve matters through internal grievance procedures, and all have failed. Being narcissistic and arrogant, bullies tend to forget that their targets have the power of speech; when they talk to each other, a whole new light is shed upon their workplace torment. Thus, class action lawsuits are instituted by several plaintiffs regarding the behavior of the same organization and bully. A petition in a class action suit would look something like this:

Jane Doe, Rowena Doe, Martin Doe, Ralph Doe, and Jack Doe
v.
Acme Organization and John Doe

Blacklisting by defaming employers and bosses is illegal if either or both make false statements about a former employee that prevents them from getting a new job. Such false statements include misrepresentations by any act, suggestion, or innuendo that result in a potential new employer not hiring a former organizational employee. In fact, misleading or false defamatory acts need not be either spoken or written; gestures, tone of voice, and other types of body language that cast aspersions on the former employee constitute blacklisting. The difficulty in blacklisting cases is that they are hard to prove. Bullies may be toxic but they are not stupid; they know the ropes and take care not to overtly blacklist a departed target in a manner that can be definitively proven. Past employers and bosses are only allowed to disclose truthful reasons why the employee quit or was fired only if they are specifically asked, and without prompting. If a former employer or boss volunteers information about the circumstances of an employee's departure from the organization, this is an actionable civil tort that, if the case is lost by the former employer or boss, can be liable to the plaintiff for triple damages.

Targets who are considering suing a defaming boss that causes intentional emotional distress should heed the following tips:

- Hire a lawyer. This book is not intended to provide legal advice; although the author has extensive legal education experience in the civil, criminal, and juvenile justice systems, this is no substitute for the advice and assistance of an attorney.

- The facts of the target's case must indicate that the plaintiff (target) suffered humiliation or great distress, especially if the plaintiff requires medical attention as a result of his or her distress.

- The facts must prove that all incidents involved business disputes such as conduct by the defendant bully in the workplace.

- The plaintiff's mental state must be the result of either (1) the defendant's intention to cause the plaintiff emotional distress, (2) the defendant knew with substantial certainty that the plaintiff would suffer emotional distress even if the defendant did not wish to cause it, and (3) the defendant recklessly disregarded the possibility that severe distress would be the result of his or her actions and did the actions anyway.

Organizations, both private and governmental, hold extreme power in our capitalistic society; upon them lies the financial security of our nation. Legislators are hesitant to institute antibullying laws and if they do, judges are slow to enforce them. Therefore, grassroots groups are the most effective way of establishing punishment for workplace bullying. It was for this reason that the Workplace Bullying Trauma Institute, headed by Namie & Namie, fired a salvo at California lawmakers. In February 2003, the Institute introduced Bill AB 1582. This bill proposes that mental and physical health impairment should extend to all employees, not just those with protective status, who seek civil court remedies for being subjected to bullying in the workplace. This bill would make it unlawful for employers or bosses to subject another employee to malicious and repeated verbal abuse, or engage in threatening, intimidating behavior and to sabotage and undermine an employee's work performance. This bill also would punish retaliation upon an employee who files grievances or lawsuits, as well as for testifying, assisting, or participating in an investigation of a bullying target's allegations.

The term vicarious liability means that top-level managers are just as culpable as the bullies in creating a toxic workplace since managers and supervisors act as agents of the organization. Top employers must investigate the grievances of bullying targets or they too can be defendants in a target's lawsuit. To sever themselves from co-liability along with the bully, employers must prove that they were aware of the target's situation and did everything possible to prevent its recurrence. Since top-level managers did not obtain their positions of power and authority by being irresponsible idiots, chances are that they will take antibullying legislation seriously if they want to avoid being in court for the rest of their natural lives and paying out huge damages to bullying targets.

California's Bill AB 1582 is the first American antibullying legislation of its kind. If it is successful, it puts other states on notice that workers' rights can be strictly enforced. Readers can check the status of this bill by going to the Web site **www.bullyinginstitute.org**. Without such laws, workplace bullying will continue unabated. Organizations will continue to discount, discredit, and deny a bullying target's grievances. There is an old lawyer's saying that if you have the facts on your side, you pound the facts. If you have the law on your side, you pound the law. If you have neither the law nor the facts on your side, you pound the table. In the hate-filled environment of workplace bullying, the facts are evident, but the law is inadequate. The pitfall of bullying cases is that there is currently no legislation in effect that acknowledges the horrific facts of workplace bullying and allows for civil tort action for defamation and other unlawful practices within an organization. Legal accountability is the only thing that will eliminate workplace bullying.

Chapter 8

Workplace Violence

When an incident of workplace violence occurs, the public is keen to know what precipitated the event. Was this the desperate action of a mentally ill person? Perhaps the perpetrator had a grudge against the organization — a disgruntled employee. In the context of this book, conceivably the perpetrator was the target of unbearable workplace bullying who simply "snapped" as a result of organizational complicity or indifference. Desperate circumstances call for desperate remedies in the eyes of perpetrators of workplace violence. Since the 1980s when a postal worker in Edmond, Oklahoma walked into his post office workplace and opened fire, the term "going postal" has become part of America's vernacular lexicon for workplace violence. Of course, there are many reasons why workplace violence occurs, but this book confines itself to the correlation between workplace bullying and workplace violence.

CASE STUDY: THE FAIRCHILD INCIDENT

On a sunny day at Fairchild Air Force Base, a young airman with a documented history of mental health issues entered the mental health section at Fairchild and opened fire with an automatic weapon. He was extremely agitated at being recommended for discharge by personnel at Fairchild.

The airman went first for the psychiatrist who sent him to the mental health

CASE STUDY: THE FAIRCHILD INCIDENT

clinic at the USAF's largest hospital in San Antonio, Texas. After mortally wounding the psychiatrist, the airman also killed the clinic's psychologist who had been involved in his case. Only the staff clinical social worker was left alive because he barricaded his office door with his metal desk and then hid under it. The airman exited the medical group and was shot and killed by a Security Forces troop. In documents released under the Freedom of Information Act, this airman felt that he was being unfairly "railroaded" into being discharged from the military by those who had power over him.

Workplace violence is generally defined as any physical assault, threatening behavior, or verbal abuse within a work setting. Spreading rumors, verbal abuse, stupid pranks, arguments, psychological trauma, sabotage, and anger-related incidents all can lead to violence by a current or past employee who has had enough. Workplace violence includes:

- Beatings

- Stabbings

- Suicides

- Shootings

- Rapes

- Attempted suicides

- Psychological traumas

- Threats

- Intimidation

- Harassment of any type

- Being followed, spied on, or stalked

- Occurring in company buildings, parking lots, field locations, private homes, and traveling to and from the workplace

Homicide is the second leading cause of death in the workplace, with the first being industrial accidents. Assaults and threats of violence number close to two million per year. Types of workplace violence include the "out of nowhere" violence by strangers, violence by customers, and violence by workers. It is difficult to predict an employee's violence, but the U.S. and Canada have formulated a checklist of warning signs that an employee may become violent, particularly in workplace bullying:

- Small incidents escalate to physical or emotional violence

- An employee shows a distinct change in his or her behavior patterns

- Crying, sulking, or temper tantrums by the employee

- Disregard for policies on absenteeism or lateness

- Disrespect for authority figures, including the bullying boss

- Decrease in the employee's satisfactory work performance

- Faulty decision-making

- Profanity and/or emotional language

- Overreaction to criticism

- Forgetfulness, confusion, and distraction from job tasks

- Inability to focus

- Blaming others for the target's mistakes

- Complaints of unfair treatment that do not resolve in the target's favor

- Insistence that the target is always right

- Personal hygiene is poor or ignored

- Sudden changes in the employee's energy level to complete tasks

- Complaints of unusual or nonspecific stress-related illnesses

An employee cannot be fired based solely on what he or she might do, but on what he or she actually says or does. Yet if an organization's worker(s) notices that a bullying target states his intention to harm another employee and holds an intense grudge against a boss or supervisor, this is a red flag that violence may erupt in the workplace. The targeted employee may utter escalating threats of violence and seem preoccupied with violence toward the organization or the bullying boss. The employee may display unusual anger and argumentative behavior. He or she may, by this time, be hypersensitive of criticism. The target may feel singled out, humiliated, and have an exceedingly low self-esteem — possibly from prolonged bullying. Extreme or bizarre behavior that is unusual for the bullying target can cause alarm among coworkers. The employee may have a history of dysfunctional family issues and problems with chemical dependency.

CASE STUDY: MELISSA

"I'm here because my assbag boss told me to come and my husband said that I should work through my problems in my workplace without killing anyone," said Melissa. "There is nothing I would like more than killing this moron slowly so he could feel the same pain that I've felt since I started working for him. I filed grievances, but the brass doesn't give a shit about the lower people on the totem pole."

"I've been thinking about suicide for about six months; any moment is better than this moment. I just wanted out, and I wanted them to suffer because of my death since they didn't give a damn about my life. One night, I dressed myself all in black, grabbed a bunch of sharp kitchen knives, and was ready to perform an 'Edward Scissorhands' on everyone who has (expletive) me over in that workplace. If I was going down, so were they. No one gave a damn what had been done to me, so they would suffer as I suffered. I was headed out the door when something stopped me. I don't really know what it was; just call it a realization that those who inflict pain on others will answer for it in God's judgment, not mine.

"The mortal world isn't governed by honesty and decency; it's a hotbed for those who have to be in power over others regardless of the cost. As much as I would have enjoyed cutting their throats and watching them slowly die, knowing that it was me who killed them, I stopped. They killed me emotionally, but if I retaliated against them and left their children without a parent, I was no better than they were. I still wish them dead, but it will be at someone else's act, not mine. I stopped myself from cutting their throats and laughing at their death because I had faith that they would reap what they sowed. I'm better than they are."

Melissa's story is not uncommon among employees, particularly targets of bullying. Her homicidal intentions toward her bully and the organization that condoned his actions were brought about by her understandable feelings that they deserved to die. Melissa was content to act as judge, jury, and executioner of those in the workplace who had bullied and betrayed her. Melissa may have stopped herself from committing homicidal workplace violence based upon her internal values and morals, but many others have not. Being the target of constant bullying, especially mob bullying, is a prime factor in predicting workplace violence. When bullying becomes deadly, there are several identified risk factors:

- Possession of handguns by traumatized targets of bullying

- Increased use of the justice system for complaints against the bully

- A history of violent thoughts documented by mental health practitioners

- Unrestricted movement by the target within the community and organization

- An increase in an employee's use of physical and emotional assistance by experts

- Isolation of the target within the organization

- A known history of alcohol or drug abuse by the employee

- Persistent claims of being treated unfairly by bosses and managers

- Blaming others in the workplace for personal problems

- Making statements that he or she wants something bad to happen to their boss

- Increased absenteeism

- Escalating alcohol and other drug abuse

- History of previous threats of violence toward coworkers or bosses

- Quiet, seething, sullen behavior

- Sudden mood swings

- Refusal to comply with policies and refusal to perform tasks

The National Institute for Occupational Safety and Health (NIOSH) published a "Homicide Alert" in May 1995. This alert was one of the first of its kind. It contained information on high-risk occupations and workplaces, informed employers and employees about risk factors, and encouraged employers to evaluate risk factors in their workplace and implement protective measures against workplace violence. NIOSH compiled the following information about the victims of workplace violence:

- 80 percent are male

- 50 percent are between the ages of 25 and 44; 50 percent are 65 or older

- 75 percent are Caucasian

- 75 percent were killed with firearms

Since NIOSH's original 1995 alert, a current profile of employees indicates that most perpetrators are white males, age 25-35, who have a history of unhappiness within the company that borders on being paranoid delusional. Most often, they have serious interpersonal difficulties with managers and supervisors in the workplace and document each incident of conflict with bosses, including the manner in which the boss treats them. Perpetrators are often isolated from other employees and have difficulty handling stress during an organization's high-productivity period. Some have mental health problems like depression, anxiety or personality disorders. Perpetrators almost always verbalize a vague reference of their intention to harm others to at least one other coworker. They often have difficulty expressing anger appropriately, and use abusive language when speaking of their boss to others. They are observed by coworkers to shout, throw objects, punch walls, and slam doors.

> *"He built up his resentment against his boss over the past year. I was really afraid something like this would happen, but he denied thinking of hurting anyone whenever I asked him. He finally couldn't take it anymore. Now he and four other people are dead because no one would listen when he tried to talk about being harassed on the job."*
> **—Sharon, wife of a perpetrator of workplace violence**

A crucial legal matter warrants explanation here: the concept of duty to warn in civil tort law.

Mental health clinicians often treat patients who have problems with anger, personality disorders, and violent fantasies about hurting those who have hurt them emotionally, economically, physically, or socially. In every mental health profession, there is a specific required code of ethical conduct toward patients; the primary ethic is confidentiality. No clinician can speak about or release case files of a client without his or her permission. Failure to follow this code can result in suspension or forfeiture of the clinician's license to practice.

There is only one exception to the code of confidentiality: the duty to warn others if a patient expresses an intention to harm them and has a specific plan to do so. In the precedent-setting case of *Tarasoff v. Regents of the University of California,* Prosenjit Poddar was receiving psychological care in the university's counseling center. He told his two clinicians that he intended to kill Tatiana Tarasoff. The clinicians asked the campus police to detain Poddar, but they released him because he seemed rational. The clinicians did not warn Tarasoff or her parents. Two months later, Poddar did indeed kill Tatiana Tarasoff. Her parents brought a civil tort action of wrongful death against the two clinicians. In 1976, the Supreme Court ruled that the special relationship between Poddar and his psychologist was special, and that it created a duty to warn third parties if they believe that lives are in danger. The clinicians, the Court held, should have warned Tatiana or her parents that Poddar expressed a plan to kill her. Since the campus police had no special relationship with Poddar, they had no duty to warn.

The Tarasoff case has become the law of the land, known by all mental health practitioners. It is an exception to codes of ethics; confidentiality does not apply when, under Tarasoff, a clinician has a duty to warn another party that a patient plans to kill him or her. Targets of workplace bullying often seek therapy services to cope with their situations. If a target expresses fantasies about killing the bullying boss, the therapist has no duty to warn the boss, but should explore these fantasies further. If a target expresses an actual intention and a plan to kill his or her boss, Tarasoff's duty to warn does apply; the therapist must inform the boss that the target intends to kill him and he or she is advised to take precautionary measures. In virtually all cases, the target would be committed to a secure psychiatric facility where he or she can receive treatment, and the intended victim remain safe.

To prevent bully-related workplace violence, the following recommendations apply:

- An organization must establish a zero-tolerance policy against bullying and strictly enforce it. Create the no asshole rule.

- All personnel should be encouraged to speak confidentially to a manager they trust about suspicions that a bullying target intends to harm the bully and possibly upper management.

- All personnel should be annually briefed, verbally and in writing, on the warning signs of possible workplace violence.

- Upper managers should take every allegation of bullying seriously and thoroughly follow up and document these reports.

- Mental health professionals that work within the organization must comply with the Tarasoff duty to warn bullying bosses that they are in danger by the target.

- Upper management should make high-risk areas like parking garages and basements more visible to others and have good lighting fixtures.

- Within each workplace, silent alarms should be installed that are accessible to all employees.

- Maintain security checkpoints with metal detectors at all entry points.

- Provide training in conflict resolution and mediation.

- Install bulletproof glass in mostly glass work stations.

- Provide random security personnel "walk arounds."

- Establish, communicate, and practice emergency responses if a violent situation erupts.

- Eliminate provocative asshole bullies from the organization, including mobbers.

- Value all employees equally; take care of them and they will take care of the company.

Unless an employee is seriously mentally ill, as in schizophrenia or other psychotic disorders, workplace violence can be prevented. Like school shootings, all it takes is acknowledgement of the problem and taking action to solve the problem. The world can be a dangerous place and people have the need and the right to feel safe in their own homes and their workplaces.

"I am a civilized person who detests violence. But during this experience, I did say to my mother and a couple of close friends, 'Now I know how those postal workers feel when they walk in and spray the place with bullets. Because I am that angry.'"

Joan, a mobbing victim
From Davenport et al.

Conclusion

Maya Angelou once said, "You did what you knew at the time. When you knew better, you did better." This wisdom can be applied to upper-level organization managers, midlevel managers and supervisors, and all workers at all levels. No matter how hard you pound a pancake, it still has two sides; many victims of workplace bullying feel that their side is either never heard or that it is disregarded. Siobhan's case makes exactly this point; when her attorney tried to tell the new upper-level boss about her mob bullying situation, he interrupted and said, "We're just going to get rid of her." These are the kinds of situations where workplace violence can erupt. A closer examination of her situation makes one wonder why her mob bullies are still alive.

If top managers and CEOs wonder why work productivity is decreasing, morale among employees is poor, there is a steady increase of sick leave and absenteeism, the staff turnover rate is increasing, and an unusual number of grievances are filed against one individual manager, they may have an "Aha!" moment when it occurs to them that they may have a bullying asshole in their midst who is sabotaging the organization's mission. This may be followed by what writer Stephen King dubbed an "Oh, shit!" moment when upper managers have a flash of understanding of how just one bully can wreak havoc in the workplace. Unfortunately, both of these moments are few and far between due to the lack of antibullying legislation. Nevertheless, this should not prevent organizations, on their own volition, from establishing strict antibullying policies. Not only is this the smart way of doing business, it is also the humane way to treat targets of bullying. There are numerous training programs on workplace bullying for interested top managers; finding this information on the Internet is easy.

No employee should be made to endure disrespectful treatment, the loss of their self-esteem and reputation, and the physical and emotional fallout of being constantly bullied. It is the target that is driven from the job by the bully or bullies, when it should be the bullies who should be driven out for the sake of the organization and its workers. If top managers have received crucial training about workplace bullying, they will find it easy to determine that serial bullies and mobbers are pathological people; their presence in the workplace is a liability to any organization. The smartest and most humane thing that upper managers can do for their organization is to stop protecting bullies and tell them to either stop or get out.

Bullying in the military is a unique problem, and the time has come for it to be addressed by the armed forces Chiefs of Staff, Surgeons General, HQ of the Inspectors General, and HQ of the Staff Judge Advocates (government attorneys). The Uniform Code of Military Justice should be revised to hold bullying commanders and workplace mobbers accountable for their actions even to the point of convening a court martial for the worst offenders. As Devin's case illustrated, military senior personnel should no longer be allowed to hide their bullying under the excuse of "good order and discipline." Without these changes, the armed forces will continue to be organizations that are safe harbors for bullies and mobbers, resulting in fewer military personnel to defend

America's way of life. Our defense posture will be diminished, our power threatened, and our defenders will gradually become fewer.

The term "disgruntled employee" is offensive, overused, and erroneously used to dismiss the claims by targets that they are being bullied in their workplaces. The term is used as an excuse by organizational management for not hearing or heeding a target's legitimate complaints. Like the "F" and "N" words, this term should be erased from the organizational, media, and legal lexicon. Targets of bullying are indeed disgruntled and for good reason. Instead of using this derogatory term to ignore a target's bullying, upper-level managers, attorneys, and media personnel should describe targets who have resorted to lawsuits and even workplace violence as "alleged victims of workplace bullying." It is time to call it what it is as an alternative for disrespecting and blaming the target.

Grassroots organizations should continue unabated to lobby for antibullying legislation. Congressmen are elected public officials and serve only at the will of the public. Every person should contact their congressmen and those running for office to explain their stance on antibullying legislation. A sample petition is included in this book's appendix. By enacting such legislation, America would be putting into practice Dr. P. C. McGraw's concept that we must teach people how to treat us.

Targets of workplace bullies who receive no relief from upper management should "go public." The most effective way to put rats on the run is to shine the spotlight on them. When all internal grievance procedures have been ignored, targets should tell their story to the media in a variety of forms, from letters to the editors of newspapers, through lawsuits for defamation and other torts discussed in this book, to public speaking engagements. Instead of slinking away in undeserved shame that is caused by the bully and the organization who tolerates or colludes with him or her, targets should hold themselves proudly and cry "foul" until someone listens and takes action against workplace bullying.

The 23 million employees who report that they are, or have been, bullying targets cannot all be mentally ill or "disgruntled." It is time for America to take a stand for human dignity and decent treatment in the workplace. We live in a society that seems contradictory at times; we decry victimization in other countries, yet we do nothing to prevent the physical and emotional agony of our own workers. Our own hands are not clean. Let us tend to our own house before we intervene in the injustices in other countries.

To conclude this book on a personal note, this author understands pathological mob bullying only too well. As a former target, the author will no longer remain silent because of shame, guilt, and poor self-esteem. By writing this book, the author proudly joins others who seek an end to the vicious practice of bullying in the workplace. Any target who has a legitimate case of bullying victimization must speak out instead of nursing his wounds in silence. This author understands them and joins them in this struggle to force organizations and lawmakers to do the right thing.

We are not going away.

Appendix

Dr. Heinz Leymann's Typology

First Category: Impact on Self-Expression and the Way Communication Happens

1) Your superior restricts the opportunity for you to express yourself.

2) You are constantly interrupted.

3) Colleagues and coworkers restrict your opportunity to express yourself.

4) You are yelled at and loudly scolded.

5) Your work is constantly criticized.

6) There is constant criticism about your personal life.

7) You are terrorized on the telephone.

8) Oral threats are made.

9) Written threats are sent.

10) Contact is denied through looks or gestures.

11) Contact is denied through innuendo.

Secondary Category: Attacks on Your Social Relations

1) People do not speak with you anymore.

2) You cannot talk to anyone; access to others is denied.

3) Colleagues are forbidden to talk with you.

4) You are treated as if you are invisible.

Third Category: Attacks on Your Reputation

1) People talk badly about you behind your back.

2) Unfounded rumors about you are circulated.

3) You are ridiculed.

4) You are treated as if you are mentally ill.

5) You are forced to undergo a psychiatric evaluation.

6) Your handicap is ridiculed.

7) People imitate your gestures, walk, or voice to ridicule you.

8) Your political or religious beliefs are ridiculed.

9) Your private life is ridiculed.

10) Your nationality is ridiculed.

11) You are forced to do a job that affects your self-esteem.

12) Your efforts are judged in a wrong and demeaning way.

13) Your decisions are always questioned.

14) You are called by demeaning names.

15) Sexual innuendoes are present.

Fourth Category: Attacks on the Quality of Your Professional and Life Situation

1) There are no special tasks for you.

2) Supervisors take away assignments, so you cannot invent new tasks to do.

3) You are given meaningless jobs to carry out.

4) You are given jobs that are below your qualifications.

5) You are continually given new tasks.

6) You are given tasks that affect your self-esteem.

7) You are given tasks that are way beyond your qualifications in order to discredit you.

8) Causing general damages that create financial costs to you.

9) Damaging your home or workplace.

Fifth Category: Direct Attacks on Your Health

1) You are forced to do a physically strenuous job.

2) Threats of physical violence are made.

3) Light violence is used to threaten you.

4) Physical abuse is present.

5) Outright sexual harassment is present.

Appeals to Lawmakers

Employment Relationships: Law and Practice

Dear (Congressman's Name)

Bullying is an emotional assault in every American workplace that has not yet been recognized as a cause of action separate from discrimination against persons of a protected status. Consequently, there are no laws that explicitly deal with this type of injury. Research indicates that 23 million American workers have — or are still — suffered being bullied in the workplace.

Victims of workplace bullying are insufficiently protected, even though these cases could be dealt with under a number of legal arguments such as defamation, wrongful termination, and constructive discharge. Yet the victims of workplace bullying currently have no specific remedy in the civil tort courts. Bullying can happen to anyone; individuals not categorized as having protective status should be allowed to sue under a civil tort law designed particularly for workplace bullying.

Therefore, it is crucial that lawmakers educate themselves about workplace bullying and its traumatic devastation upon bullying targets. Please consider passing legislation that specifies the circumstances of bullying in the workplace, recognizes the serious emotional and physical illnesses caused by targets of bullying, serves as a preventative instrument, and constitutes a better protection for targets of bullying.

New legislation should be instituted that shapes legal consequences for workplace bullies and the top-level managers of an organization who are either unaware of the business costs of bullying, act in collusion with bullies, or don't care about the consequences that bullying has upon their employees.

Sincerely,

Your Name

Example of a Workplace Bullying Policy

(Company name) considers workplace bullying unacceptable and will not tolerate it under any circumstances. Workplace bullying is behavior that harms, intimidates, offends, degrades, or humiliates an employee, possibly in front of other employees and customers. Workplace bullying causes the loss of trained and talented personnel, reduces productivity and morale, and creates legal risks of liability on behalf of the bullied employee.

(Company's name) believes that all employees should be able to work in a bullying-free environment. Managers and supervisors must ensure that employees are fairly evaluated but not bullied.

(Company's name) has internal grievance and investigative procedures to deal with workplace bullying. Any reports of bullying will be treated seriously and promptly investigated in a confidential and impartial manner.

(Company's name) encourages all employees to report incidents of workplace bullying. Managers and supervisors must ensure that all employees who make complaints or who sue for damages are not retaliated against or victimized.

Prompt and decisive action will be taken against anyone who bullies an employee. Discipline may involve a warning, transfer, counseling, and demotion or dismissal based upon the circumstances.

(Company's name) has established the contact person for reports of workplace bullying. That person is (name and phone number).

Example of a Military Member's Request for Antibullying Laws Under the Uniform Code of Military Justice

(By Author)

Memorandum To: (name of Surgeon General or Chief of Staff)

Date:

My name is (insert name and rank, branch of service). I am a target of workplace bullying in my duty station. I have been (bullied or mob bullied) for the past (time). I have used all internal grievance procedures to eliminate bullying, such as the Inspector General and congressional inquiries.

To date, I have received no relief from these internal and congressional complaints because of the protection that military commanders use as being relevant to "good order and discipline." Nevertheless, the bullying that I was, and/or am, subjected to continues unabated and clearly outside the scope of their authority. I believe that the (service branch) protects the illegal and abusive acts of bullying commanders and/or supervisors rather than acknowledging and punishing their actions that are clearly beyond the scope of their duties and are maliciously motivated.

I call upon the (Chief of Service Branch and the Surgeon General) to actively curtail workplace bullying in the military through the Uniform Code of Military Justice. Bullying commanders, supervisors, and coworkers must be held accountable for their inappropriate bullying tactics, and be subject to punishment under the UCMJ.

Respectfully,

(service member's name, rank and branch of service)

Self-Assessment: Are You a Bullying Asshole?

(S. Samenow, 2004)

Instructions: Indicate if, in your opinion, each statement is true or false, depending upon your typical feelings and interactions with the people in your workplace.

1) Do you feel surrounded by incompetent idiots, and you need to let them know the truth about them now and then?

2) You were a nice person until you started working with a bunch of incompetent creeps.

3) You do not trust the people around you, and they don't trust you.

4) You see your coworkers and subordinates as competitors.

5) You believe that the best way to climb the ladder of success is to push people out of your way.

6) You secretly enjoy watching other people suffer.

7) You are often jealous of your colleagues and subordinates' abilities and find it difficult to compliment them on their work.

8) You have a small list of close friends and a long list of enemies; you are proud of both.

9) You sometimes cannot contain your contempt toward

losers and jerks in your workplace.

10) You like to glare at, insult and sometimes holler at some of the idiots in your workplace to make them shape up.

11) You take credit for the accomplishments of your team because they are too incompetent to succeed without your intervention.

12) You enjoy firing comments in meetings that humiliate other employees.

13) You rapidly point out the mistakes of your subordinates.

14) You do not make mistakes. When something goes wrong, you find a target to blame.

15) You constantly interrupt employees because what you have to say is much more important.

16) You constantly soothe your own boss, and expect the same loyalty from the subordinates that you bully.

17) Your jokes and teasing about an employee can be subliminally nasty at times.

18) You are constantly engaged in warfare with your employees. You treat everyone like crap; employees are either "in" or "in the way."

19) You notice that people avoid eye contact with you and seem nervous when they speak with you.

20) You have the feeling that people are always cautious about what they say to you.

21) People respond to your e-mails in a "flaming" manner and with hostile reactions.

22) People are hesitant to talk with you about personal information because they seem to be reluctant to trust you.

23) People stop having fun when you're around.

24) People react to your arrival by announcing that they have to leave company social events.

Key:

0-5 true answers means that you may not be a certified asshole unless you are fooling yourself by not answering the questions truthfully.

5-15 true answers means that you appear to be a borderline asshole who needs to change his or her behavior before it is too late.

15 or more true answers means that you are a full-blown bullying asshole; get help immediately or face termination.

Self-Assessment: How Bullying Affects You

(Adapted from Namie & Namie)

Exercise #1

You have learned how to recognize workplace bullying. This exercise will help you learn how to counter the bully's false accusations so you can remind yourself of just how competent you truly are. There are four areas about you that you, your friends, families, and coworkers (those whom you can trust) can evaluate:

- **How I Relate to Others**

  Descriptions of strengths and weakness in relationship with friends and coworkers.

- **How Other People See Me**

  Do you get along with others? Are you seen as an angry person? Are you helpful to others? Are you shy?

- **My Performance at Work**

  Describe the way you handle job assignments. Are you on time? Are you a procrastinator? Are you a "neatnik" or a workaholic?

- **My Ability to Reason and Solve Problems**

  Do you like having the freedom to improvise? Are you a quick learner? Do you have special knowledge in certain areas?

Take some private, quiet time to write down as many phrases about yourself that you can think of. Be totally honest; do not be shy, too critical, or humble. Do not write anything that the bully or bullies have said about you because they are manipulative liars. Make at least two copies of this exercise and give one to a friend and one to a family member. Tell them to be honest also; your feelings will not be hurt by anything they write. When all three of you are finished, lay the sheets side by side. Do you see similarities? What are your strengths? Do you judge yourself too harshly? Write down what you learned from this exercise that helps make you bully-proof.

Exercise #2

This exercise is another way of evaluating how bully-proof you are. It is extremely useful in helping you cope with any type of workplace bullying without it paralyzing your thoughts and emotions about yourself.

- The quality of your relationships with others. This is an indicator of how the bully has poisoned the good relationships that you have with others, including coworkers and friends. Are you isolating yourself from others out of shame, fear, or lack of confidence in yourself?

- Confidence in your personal competence. Gain insight into how you react to stress, criticism from the bully or mobbers, and respond to being bullied. The erosion of your self-confidence and feelings of competence is the goal of bullies; once lost, it is difficult to regain. On a scale of one to ten, rate your personal competence, and then write down what you can do to take back what was stolen from you by bullies and mobbers.

- Emotional effectiveness. Too much or too little emotion can be a problem for you. Write down how the bullies or mobbers have harmed your ability to feel, instead of emotional numbness. Then write down how you can return to a comfortable way of expressing your emotions.

Celebrity Bad Bosses

Scott Ruden is a film producer, whose credits include *The Queen*, *The Royal Tenenbaums*, and *The Firm*. According to *The Wall Street Journal*, Ruden has fired as many as 250 personnel assistants; he fired one assistant for bringing him the wrong kind of breakfast muffin.

Naomi Campbell is a supermodel with a super ego to match. If not handled carefully, she may cause bodily harm to others. In 2007, Campbell pleaded guilty to misdemeanor assault for hitting her housekeeper with a cell phone over a pair of missing jeans. She insisted that this incident was accidental, but she has a history of similar events, including a 2000 guilty plea for assaulting a personal assistant on a movie set, which indicates otherwise.

Simon Cowell, the mastermind behind *American Idol*, has notoriously high standards for which he is unapologetic. Cowell is known for finding new and creative ways to insult everyone from contestants to show host Ryan Seacrest. He appears to relish his reputation as the "Idol" judge that everyone loves to hate. It is his prickly personality that made him famous.

Al Capone is a name synonymous with organized crime in the United States during the Prohibition years. He was well known for his involvement with selling illegal whiskey, gambling, and prostitution as well as for his brutality, even toward his own mob. He ordered the "hit" on Bugs Moran and his men in the St. Valentine's Day massacre in 1929. After serving eight years in prison for tax evasion, Capone retired to his Florida estate where, in 1947, he died from complications of syphilis.

Leona Helmsley, now deceased, was the Manhattan hotelier who will go down in history as "The Queen of Mean." She earned this nickname because of her angry, erratic behavior and hasty firing of employees. Helmsley once said, "Only little people pay taxes," and she served time in prison for tax evasion. In 2004, she was ordered by a court to pay a former landscaper for breach of contract; she fired the landscaper after learning that he was gay.

Gordon Ramsay is a hot-tempered chef and host of *Hell's Kitchen*. He never holds back when it comes to doling out criticism, but Ramsay spices up his tirades with profanity about anything or anyone who displeases him.

Little Miss Can't-Be-Wrong

(from *Slate* Magazine's Advice Column)

Dear Prudence,

I'm an office manager at a very small company, where I work with three other girls. In short, I am much smarter than my co-workers. When one of them asks a dumb question (i.e., "What's so bad about Fox News?"), I try to be sensitive and explain without making them feel stupid. Sometimes, though, I get very frustrated, and it's difficult to hold my tongue. Yesterday, my co-worker's sister came in to visit and announced shamelessly that she had never heard of Craigslist. After she left, I exclaimed to my other co-workers "I can't believe she's never heard of Craigslist!" My co-workers defended her, saying they had never heard of Craigslist until they moved to New York City. I find this preposterous. I didn't say anything else because I didn't want to come off as a snob (which is probably how I am coming off in this e-mail; my apologies). How does one handle working with people like this? I could keep my mouth shut and go with the flow, but it makes me feel dumb when I don't speak up — I feel that if I don't acknowledge their stupidity, then I'm not doing my duty as an informed young woman.

—Dumbed Down

Dear Dumbed,

Since you're so knowledgeable, I'll leave it to you to answer the following letter:

Dear Prudie,

The three of us work in a small office with an overbearing braggart who thinks it's her job to constantly tell us how smart she is and how dumb we are. If we say something that indicates we don't agree with her political views, she rolls her eyes and gives us a lecture on how to think. If it comes up that we don't know about some Web site she's familiar with, for example, she sighs and tells us it's impossible to believe that we could be that unsophisticated. Her attitude almost seems to be that she feels it's her obligation to point out how superior she is. In some small way, we feel sorry for her because she's so unlikeable, but mostly we just can't bear the sight of her. How do we get her to shut up?

— Sick of the Show-Off

"Failing to confront costs a procrastinating target and the family more than the worst imagined consequence."

— Namie & Namie

Bibliography

Adler, A. (1938). *Social Interest: A Challenge to Mankind*. Boston, MA: Oneworld Publications.

American Psychiatric Association. (2000). *Diagnostic and Statistical Manual of Mental Disorders* (4th ed. Text Revision). Washington, D.C.: Author.

Babiak, P., and Hare, R. (2007). *Snakes in Suits: When Psychopaths go to Work*. Boston, MA: Collins.

Cade, V. (August 25, 2007). "How to Have a Bully Free Workplace." Retrieved September 19, 2007 from *How to Have a Bully Free Workplace*: **www.howtohaveabullyfreeworkplace.com.**

Cavaiola, A., and Lavender, N. (2000). *Toxic Coworkers*. Oakland, CA: New Harbinger Publications.

Davenport, N., Schwartz, R., and Elliott, G. (1999). *Mobbing: Emotional Abuse in the American Workplace*. Ames, IA: Civil Society Publishing.

Devine, T. (November 15, 2007). "Workplace Bullying Institute: Whistleblower's Checklist." Retrieved November 19, 2007 from **www.bullyinginstitute.org**.

Emanuel, S. L. (2002). Emanuel Law Outlines. *Torts*. New York: Aspen Publishers, Inc.

Futterman, S. (2004). *When You Work for a Bully*. Montvale, NJ: Croce Publishing Group, LLC.

Hare, R. (1993). *Without Conscience: The Disturbing World of the Psycopaths Among Us*. New York: Pocket Books.

Hurd, David. (2007). "Defamation and Blacklisting." Retrieved November 22, 2007 from **www.bullyinginstitute.org.**

Kohut, M. (2002). Powerpoint presentation: "Understanding the Personality Disorders." Retrieved October 13, 2007 from Rocky Mountain Way Freelance Writing.

Kohut, M. (2004). PowerPoint presentation: "Workplace Violence." Retrieved October 13, 2007 from Rocky Mountain Way Freelance Writing.

Kohut, M. (2004). PowerPoint presentation: "Yours Truly, Jack the Ripper." Retrieved November 2, 2007 from Rocky Mountain Way Freelance Writing.

Leman, R. (2007). Canada's National Occupational Health & Safety Resource. Retrieved October 7, 2007 from **www.cchohs. ca.**

Lorenz, M. (October 22, 2007). "Celebrity Bad Bosses." Retrieved November 25, 2007 from **www.careerbuilder.com.**

Lubit, R. H. (2004). *Coping With Toxic Managers, Subordinates, and Other Difficult People*. Upper Sadle River, NJ: Prentice Hall.

McGraw, P. C. (1999). *Life Strategies*. New York: Hyperion.

Mueller, R. (2005). *Bullying Bosses: A Survival Guide*. San Francisco, CA: **www.bullyingbosses.com**.

Namie, G. (2007). "Some Success Stories." Retrieved October 12, 2007 from **www.bullyinginstitute.org.**

Namie, G., and Namie, R. (2000). *The Bully at Work*. Naperville, IL: Sourcebooks, Inc.

Prudence, D. (October 25, 2007). "Dear Prudence." In *Slate* magazine. Retrieved November 12, 2007 from **www.slate.com.**

Said, C. (January 21, 2007). "Bullying Bosses Could Be Busted." The *San Francisco Chronicle*. Retrieved September 29, 2007 from **www.SFGate.com**.

Samenow, S. (1998). *Straight Talk About Criminals*. Lanham, MD: Rowman & Littlefield.

Samenow, S. (Revised, 2004). *Inside the Criminal Mind*. New York: Crown Publishing Group.

Shapiro, R., and Jankowski, M. (2005). *Bullies, Tyrants, and Impossible People*. New York: Crown Business.

Sutton, R. (2007). *The No Asshole Rule*. New York: Warner Business Books.

U.S. Department of Labor. (2002). "OSHA Fact Sheet." Retrieved September 2, 2007 from **www.osha.gov.**

Washington State Department of Labor & Industries. "Workplace Bullying: What Everyone Needs to Know." Retrieved October 2, 2007 from **www.LNI.wa.gov.**

Wikipedia. (1999). "Workplace Bullying." Retrieved November 12, 2007 from **www.wikipedia.org.**

Author Biography

Margaret R. Kohut

Margaret Kohut is an Oklahoma native and still holds proudly onto her "Midwestern drawl." She earned college degrees in English, Criminal Justice, and a Master's degree in Social Work. Her initial foray into human service work was as a correctional officer in both adult and juvenile maximum security correctional institutions. Margaret's unique job history includes being a courtroom bailiff and a fugitive recovery agent ("bounty hunter"), and she spent a year in the private practice of clinical social work specializing in adoption studies, pre-sentence investigations, probation and parole intervention, family therapy, and therapy with troubled juveniles. Margaret has a strong educational and vocational history of forensic counseling and addiction therapy.

Margaret served in the United States Air Force for seventeen years as a commissioned officer and clinical social worker providing psychotherapy services for active duty members, family members, and retirees. Margaret served the nation during Operation Desert Storm and Operation Iraqi Freedom. She is now a disabled veteran, conducting her full-time freelance writing business from her home. Margaret maintains national-level certifications in human services, as found in her C.V. She is a prolific writer, having penned many award-winning publications for the Air Force on mental health issues, domestic violence, workplace violence, chemical dependency, trauma therapy, and adolescent acting-out behavior. As a civilian, Margaret coauthored an academic textbook on sexual serial killers and has been extensively published in the *Canadian Journal of Adlerian Psychology* and other academic publications. Margaret founded Rocky Mountain Way Freelance Writing in February 2006 after more than 20 years of noncommercial writing. Her lengthy C.V. attests to the success of her commercial writing abilities.

Margaret lives in Anaconda, Montana with her husband of 15 years, Lt. Col. (ret) Dr. Tristan Kohut, Medical Director of the Montana State Prison, and their 13 miniature Dachshunds; most of them are accomplished animal-assisted therapy dogs.

"Service to others is in my blood," Margaret says. "After the great honor of serving my country, I hope to help others through my writing and leave this world a better place than I found it."

Index

Employee Body Language Revealed: How to Predict Behavior in the Workplace by Reading and Understanding Body Language

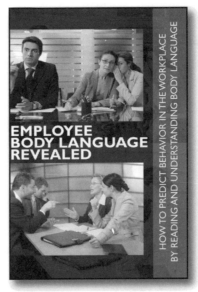

Only 7 percent of communication is verbal and 38 percent is vocal. The largest chunk then, 55 percent, is visual. People form 90 percent of their opinion about you within the first 90 seconds of meeting you. Understanding body language is a skill that can enhance your life. This understanding can be a plus in the workplace. You can know what an employee or co-worker thinks and feels by examining their subconscious body language. And, like the world's best communicators, you can have strong body language that reflects confidence, competence, and charisma.

This groundbreaking new book will make you an expert on body language. You will have the ability to read people's minds. Would you like to know if a co-worker is interested or attracted to you, when an employee or co-worker is lying or telling the truth, how to make instant friends, and persuade and influence others? This book contains proven techniques that will make people, including employers and co-workers, like you and trust you. You can use your body language to your advantage by transmitting only the messages you want people to receive. This specialized book will demonstrate step by step how to use body language to your benefit in the workplace and in everyday situations.

ISBN-10: 1-60138-147-6 • ISBN-13: 978-1-60138-147-7
288 Pages • Item # EBL-01 • $21.95

THE COMPLETE GUIDE TO UNDERSTANDING, CONTROLLING, & STOPPING BULLIES & BULLYING: A COMPLETE GUIDE FOR TEACHERS AND PARENTS

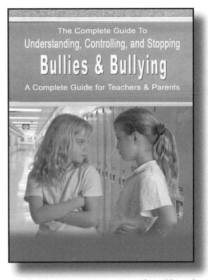

In April 2007, 32 students were killed during the Virginia Polytechnic Institute and State University shooting. According to MSNBC news services, the student gunman was bullied and mocked by his classmates.

Forty percent of U.S. students voluntarily report being involved in bullying — as bullies or as victims — according to the results of the first national survey on this subject. Bullying is increasingly viewed as an important contributor to youth violence, including homicide and suicide. Case studies of the shooting at Columbine High School and other U.S. schools trace the multiple murders to bullying incidents.

Given that most bullying goes unnoticed and unreported, Americans have been slow to react to this behavior that is taking over our schools. All children deserve the right to go to school free of intimidation. Help make your school bully-free by using the information contained in this groundbreaking new book. If you are interested in learning essentially everything there is to know about stopping bullies and bullying, then this book is for you.

ISBN-10: 1-60138-021-6 • ISBN-13: 978-1-60138-021-0
288 Pages • $24.95

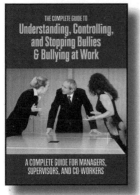